SOCIAL WORK
THROUGH
GROUP PROCESS

SOCIAL WORK
THROUGH
GROUP PROCESS

ALAN F. KLEIN

PROFESSOR OF SOCIAL WORK

SCHOOL OF SOCIAL WELFARE

STATE UNIVERSITY OF NEW YORK AT ALBANY

1970

ADDRESS ALL CORRESPONDENCE AND ORDERS TO:

Raymond F. Mahoney, Assistant Dean
School of Social Welfare
State University of New York at Albany
Albany, New York 12203

First Printing   February, 1970
Second Printing   April, 1970
Third Printing   August, 1970

Library of Congress Catalog Card Number 78-630897

HV
45
.K54

TABLE OF CONTENTS

TABLE OF CONTENTS

Quotation on page 1 from John P. Spiegel, "Campus Conflict
and Professional Egos," *Trans*-ACTION, October, 1969, p. 50.

SOCIAL WORK
THROUGH
GROUP PROCESS

"I am convinced of the necessity
of political and social change
if our society is to survive. In
my view, what needs to be changed
is the pyramidal structuring of
power in bureaucracies, and in
our communities--a stratification
that arranges persons and groups
in positions of inferiority and
superiority. Such a change, I
believe, cannot be brought about
without a simultaneous change in
values such that individualistic
achievement can no longer be used
to disguise or dilute the destructive impact of authoritarianism
and elitism in a self-advertised
democracy."

John P. Spiegel,
Director, Lemberg Center for the
Study of Violence at Brandeis
University and Professor of Social
Psychiatry at the Florence Heller
Graduate School in Social Welfare.

1

INTRODUCTION

This book is written as a supplement to the material available in the literature on social work with groups. Its major purpose is to be an aid in teaching social workers how to work with groups for social work objectives and within the boundaries of social work methods and philosophy. The book does not presume to be a text on group-work, nor a complete systematic treatment of social work with groups. Such a work would, of necessity, duplicate much useful textual and journal material.

There are gaps and omissions in the litera-ture as well as in theory. <u>Social Work through Group Process</u> is an attempt to fill some of these gaps, to add a little to theory, and, hopefully, to correct some of the distortions that inevit-ably have crept into the growing body of theory. A review of the literature of the past forty years, and especially of the last ten, reveals that social work with groups has suffered from one of the same ailments that has troubled the social sciences; namely, an adherence to mono-lithic theories, or at least an overemphasis on the part of each author on either social explana-tions or psychological analyses of the group process and the dynamics of human behavior in groups. Although for many years there has been agreement in the literature that human behavior in groups is not either/or social or psycho-logical, the leading groupwork authors still lean heavily in one or the other direction.

The introduction of general systems theory should have laid the dichotomy to rest. Its ap-plication to groupwork should certainly have made it clear that the interaction and interpenetra-tion of the subsystems of a human group preclude any simple monolithic explanation for how people behave in groups, let alone how the groupworker could proceed. Talcott Parsons made the point many years ago when he described how the person-ality system, the social system, and the cultural system interact and interpenetrate. The biolo-gists have added the physical system to the for-mulation and "psychosomatic" has become a house-hold word. In his work on field theory, Kurt

Lewin set forth the formula that behavior (B) is a function (f) of the interaction of personality (P) which includes the psychic and physical systems, the social (S) which includes the immediate social group such as reference groups, family groups, work groups, and so on, and the cultural system (C) made up of large, societal constellations with the mores, expectations, norms, et cetera of the nationality, ethnic, religious, and other such groupings to which one belongs.

Even so, today, while giving lip service to these interrelations, the major schools of thought in social work with groups not only predicate method primarily on one set of behavioral determinants, but even develop their theoretical rationale in a like manner.

It is a thesis in this book that to understand the behavior of humans in groups, both the social and the psychological frames of reference need to be utilized, but even more, they need to be viewed in interaction and not as separate determinants. Jack Douglas puts it well when he suggests that one can never understand social behavior by external factors alone. We must, he insists, study the social meanings; that is, the behavior means little until the meaning the actors give to their actions are revealed, for without the meaning there can be no understanding.[1] John Seeley goes further when he tells us that it is not valid to speak of social, psychological, or biological development as though they were discrete problems, fields, or levels of analysis. He holds that society, personality, and biological development are not related causally because, essentially, they are different ways of saying the same thing.[2]

An effort will be made in this book to demonstrate the meaning of these positions as well as to suggest how one might use the conceptualization in practice. It is the premise then that social psychologists, social scientists, or behavioral

----

[1]Jack Douglas, The Social Meanings of Suicide (Princeton: Princeton University Press, 1968).

[2]John Seeley, The Americanization of the Unconscious (New York: Science House, 1967).

3

scientists, and group therapists are not dealing
with different kinds or levels of phenomena, but
that they are using different levels of general-
izations in their explanations for the behavior of
human beings. Social work needs to view and to use
the various levels of conceptualization in the development of its own applied-practice theory. For
example, in groupwork we must accept the fact that
human effort and motivation are the major maintenance sources of almost all social structures. In
this context, human behavior in a group is clearly
at the social-psychological level. In a group, as
in a system, human beings cannot be ignored because
they furnish the sustaining input; that is, they
furnish the bond and energy.

Having said this much, it must also be noted
that the concept of partial inclusion tells us that
the group requests or requires only part of the
psychological self of the member to fulfill his
group role. Since he brings in his whole self, a
struggle goes on for the individual to maintain
his identity as a person. The "socio-behavioral"
approach to working with a group tends to deperson-
alize the member so that he can meet the role demands of the group which may not be compatible
with the personal needs of the member. This will
be discussed later in the body of the book. In
general, it is my premise that the model of groupwork predicated only on social variables tends to
run counter to the differences in individuals,
their needs for self-determination, spontaneity,
self-expression, and freedom.

I contend that the findings and conclusions
of small group research conducted within the laboratory are not valid for understanding what happens in real-life groups or organizations. Laboratory groups are under very temporary pressures
and they do not develop formal structures which
exist over a long period of time. Group structure
evolves through stages in group development wherein members share common interests derived from
common goals, from commonly held norms which grow
from working together, and from common values
which guide the behavior of the members. For the
group process to have meaning, the members must
have a stake in the outcomes. These conditions
are seldom true for experimental groups. My premise, then, is that findings in small group re-

search may be useful in social work with groups but that they are not necessarily valuable to such social work practice. The empirical studies are not to be introduced into social work with groups just because they are empirical. The studies should be examined with interest and care and where applicable be adopted. The largest percentage of published studies about groups are neither applicable nor convincing. One of the most important aspects of group dynamics, and one often neglected by the empiricist, is the concept of purpose. This, in large part, gives the framework for the organization of the segments of the book, and will be explored further.

I hold with Garland, Jones, and Kolodny that groups proceed through a sequence of stages which are characterized by the group climate or group task.[1] It seems that these stages and the emotional climate of each cannot be ignored while a group-worker is engaged in attempting to understand the structural variables, or at least that the structural variables take on new, different, and important meanings when one views them in the light of the stages of group development. The same would apply if one sought to understand the group process by analyzing only individual members, or even by confining it to the interaction of the members.

The book is divided into five sections which cannot be absolutely discrete and hence do overlap. The first section deals with concepts and theories about social work with groups. The first chapter is an overview of various approaches to groupwork in social work. It is not my purpose to describe or to explain methods but to examine the assumptions, beliefs, and positions which characterize the various approaches. Rather than deal with each author or school of thought separately, they are categorized by grouping the variables that each holds paramount, and generalizing theoretical positions from the significant vari-

---

[1]James Garland, Hubert Jones, and Ralph Kolodny, "A Model for Stages of Development in Social Work Groups," <u>Explorations in Group Work</u> (Boston: Boston University School of Social Work, 1965).

ables.

The categories are not discrete because different authors, consciously or unconsciously,
combine aspects of several positions in their
theorizing. Later in this chapter several social
groupwork writers are discussed specifically as
they, in my opinion, represent the leading authority in this field today. An effort is made, again,
to look below the surface and to seek out their
assumptions, beliefs, and positions. If the reader
is interested in the methods themselves, he is
urged to read these writers' works.

Because social action is so important, and
because lately it has been neglected in groupwork
literature, the rationale for social action is
dealt with separately.

In Chapter 2, three concepts which I believe
are of the essence are given special attention.
These are purpose, contract, and group. The first
section is a review and overview of social work
with groups as it is today. It provides the understanding which is necessary to comprehend the
groupwork model which I propose in the book.

The second section is the most important part
of the book in that it sets forth my conception
of an operating model for working with a group to
achieve social work objectives. In Chapter 3, I
have put forward as clearly as I know how my own
assumptions, beliefs, and position. It is my
hope that even if the reader does not agree with
my position, he will be able to understand and ap-
preciate it.

In order to be clear and explicit, I have elaborated on my concern that practice cannot rest
upon monolithic theories about the determinants of
human behavior. I have tried to illustrate the
interrelationship and interdependence of social
and structural elements with psychological factors
as well as to discuss group processes within the
same context. I do not attempt a unified theory
of behavior nor do I have illusions on that score.
My interest is to be illustrative and to provide
working concepts which I suggest are useful in
practice.

6

The model itself is developed in Chapter 4 under the heading "Building Blocks in Constructing a Model." This is elaborated further in the material called "The Mechanics of the Model." I have deliberately called the effort "building blocks" because I do not believe that I have fashioned a model in the real sense of that term. I do suggest that what I have put together has internal consistency, has a sound theoretical basis, is modern and up-to-date, is philosophically appropriate for social work, and that it works.

As an addendum to the model, but not part of it, I offer a "Schema for Diagnosing Group Functioning" in Chapter 5. This is presented as an aid for practitioners and not as a scientifically tight typology, I believe that it is consistent with the thesis of the working model.

Since this book is written primarily as an aid in social work education, I have written a chapter on how the student can be helped best to use the model. Chapter 6, "Notes on Field Practice," serves a dual purpose; how the student can be helped to learn to work with groups, and how the field instructor can adapt the propositions to the learning experience.

The third section is devoted to the application of social work through group process in the group services agency. Because of the current emphasis on treatment and also because groupwork has become estimable in many other kinds of social service agencies, little has been written about the traditional agency lately. Chapter 7 discusses groupwork as an appropriate methodology in the group services.

Section IV is devoted to social treatment. In Chapter 8 there is a brief discussion of the application of the model in group therapy and in family group counseling.

Section V returns to theory but now attention is given to a discriminating examination of small group theory and theory-building. In Chapter 9 I have looked critically at the current state of small group theory and have evaluated it as a viable basis for practice in social work through group process. This chapter has not been under-

taken lightly. Over the years, I have kept abreast
of the developments in small group theory and I
have searched the literature diligently in the hope
that I would find important breakthroughs that
would be applicable and would inform practice.

The final chapter in the book contains a plea
for research in groupwork conceived and designed
by social workers who have competence in group
practice. There is considerable evidence, when
one examines the experience of social work in
Europe, that when persons with little background
in practice do research, engage in policy decisions about social programs, and design community
action, for example, the results are less than
desirable. I believe that the European experience
is being confirmed in the United States.

On the other hand, practitioners who lack research skill, sophistication about policy analysis,
and are ignorant of organizational theory, are
less than ideal in social work practice. Be this
as it may, and aside from its implications for
social work education, social workers must fashion
inquiries that will solve the practical problems
involved in helping people. We cannot rely on the
methods which are current in social science research today to answer the questions that concern
us.

Alan F. Klein

Loudonville, New York
October, 1969

CHAPTER 1

ASSUMPTIONS, BELIEFS, AND POSITIONS

Human groups may be conceptualized in different ways. This is not solely a matter of definition, but also a matter of what one thinks are the parts of a group and how one thinks the parts of a group operate. One's assumptions give rise to the variables one designates and also to which of these variables one assigns significance. As a result, there are several models for groups and methods of working with groups set forth in the literature.[1]

A model is a way of stating a theory in relation to specific observations. A model is an analogue (analogous to something that is corresponding in some respects to something else) of a theory and is, therefore, specific. Models are built from theories around a problem. A model is the organization of a theory; that is, it organizes the processes and categories which appear to be related to the problem. The model, then, structures the problem and states or demonstrates what variables are explicated. A model is an analogue of a theory built to solve a problem.

A model is a problem-solving device. A theory tells one that if certain things are so, then certain other things ought to be so; but a model, granting certain things to be true, tells how certain things should happen. A model to be a model should be capable of being made into a theory. One can build a theory without building a model, but it is doubtful that one can have a model without a theory.

The term "model" does not seem to be appropriate to the current groupwork practice designs. This is true also of the attempt made by Papell and Rothman to categorize three schools of thought

[1] Catherine Papell and Beulah Rothman, "Social Group Work Models: Possession and Heritage," Journal of Education for Social Work, Vol. II, No. 2 (Fall, 1966), 66-77.

in groupwork as models. The reason they are not models is that they lack viable theories, and even more important, they fail to take into account all of the relevant variables in social work practice with groups.

We are about to examine some of the more popular designs in groupwork and even though they are not models in the true sense of the word, they are distinct schools of thought set forth in the literature. Each distinct point of view is usually attributed to a specific writer or to one school of social work. We are going to try to avoid identifying them as such and, instead, to conceptualize them in more general terms. For example, some schools of thought are predicated on the premise that social variables are the major determinants of individual behavior. They concentrate on factors that are external to the individual member. Here it is presumed that if the social variables are changed, the behavior of the individuals will change. At the other extreme, some schools prefer to think that behavior is determined by internal variables such as the "id" or the "ego" and by the internalized people and experiences in a person's life history. In such a point of view, the emphasis in social work would be upon modifying these internal variables. We will look at several more prevalent designs and comment upon them as we go along before setting forth our own preferences.

This section is in the nature of a review of the major theoretical orientations which have found favor and adherents among social workers who work with groups.

Manipulating Social Factors as a Means of Influencing Individual Behavior

It is possible to view the group as a social field. In such a context, people in a group are subject to any number of forces or influences within it. Some forces hold an individual's behavior in a steady state, others are inhibiting, and still others direct the individual's actions. The individual in the group can be likened to a cork on the waves, subject to winds and currents. To change the direction in which the cork travels, one simply changes the forces.

10

As simplistic as it may sound, there are some who believe that the behavior of individuals in a group is directed by forces external to the individual and to alter behavior one alters the external forces. It is true, undeniably, that external forces do influence behavior and that manipulation of such forces can bring about behavioral change. In such a methodology, the worker is a "change agent."

A more complex explanation for the behavior of individuals lies in viewing the group components or elements as a structure and placing the members in the structure so that the individual behavior is a result of the dynamics of the various elements in interaction. This notion is really not too different from the previous one because it still implies that the determinants of behavior lie outside of the individuals and that change results from altering the elements, the dynamics of interaction, or the location of the individual in the structure.

This conception is a popular one in groupwork today. The structural elements utilized are conceptions such as position, status, power, norm, role, and the like; the dynamics are identified as processes such as communication, boundary maintenance, goal-achieving, and so forth. To influence the social functioning of members, one alters positions, changes statuses, influences communication patterns, and so on.

Such a design can be very simple or it can be more sophisticated. Instead of viewing structure as static, that is, one's position determining in part how one will act; structure can be made up of parts in interaction so that structure is not a physical construct such as a building, a machine, a geographical area, or a molecule. It is a structure only in the sense of patterns of interaction or habitual patterns of the relationships of the parts. The structure exists only when the parts function in relation to each other. Position, for example, means location of one part in relation to other parts. Status connotes the importance of a part in relation to other parts.

If a school of thought is predicated upon

such social variables as the determinants of individual behavior, such a point of view specifies the variables which are appropriate to understanding groups and how groups work. In this conception the student would be concerned with the interdependence of the parts and how they relate to one another, and he still would be minimally interested in the parts themselves; that is, he would not seek to understand the individuals within the group. Individuals in these designs are regarded as interchangeable units whose behavior varies only because of the social conditions surrounding them. Their motivations, life experiences, or internal dynamics would not be of importance in an attempt to enhance their behavior.

There are several very popular groupwork designs today which rest their method almost exclusively on the alteration of group structure. Some groupworkers like to think that the dynamic structural construct which I have described is a systems model and as such is an advanced theoretical approach to working with a group. It is a systems model but it encompasses only one system. This means that the design is depicted as though the parts of the group system were inanimate. It ignores the individuals as living systems and too, it fails to take into account the larger system within which the group functions and which also influences the action. The larger system includes the agency, the neighborhood, the culture, and so forth.

In open systems, and human groups are open systems, the group analyst must be concerned with transaction; that is, with the relationships the group and its members have with the environment. These are designated as input from the surrounding environment and output to the environment. It should be obvious to the reader that each member-person is engaged in transactions with the group but also with the other member-persons in the group as each member constitutes part of the environment for every other member. Each member is also a system with a will. attitudes, beliefs, aptitudes, motivations, and above all, needs.

I believe that the members as well as the interactions and transactions are important considerations when doing social work through group

12

process, but the members seem to be neglected as major variables by those groupwork theorists who place primary emphasis on the social variables without regard for the psychological attributes and needs of individual members.

The concept of role has become a crucial one in the behavioral sciences, and social work has adopted it as an integrating linkage between the social and psychological frames of reference. Role is said to be the specific form of behavior required for a certain position, a status, a task; that is, standardized patterns of behavior expected or demanded regardless of personal wishes or needs. Norms sanction these role demands and usually the norms rest upon values expressed or implied. However, while role is regarded as an integrating link between psychological and social frames of reference, the concept has not matured enough to give it the full implication that it might have to explain the transaction between the person and his environment, for example, as in the group. The individual in this conceptualization has little freedom to transform his role to coincide with the expression of his personality. It seems that in some forms of practice he is persuaded, trained, or coerced into meeting the role demand and this has been called socialization, or enhancement of social functioning.

If one conceives the group in the terms described and selects the variables which go with it, then method flows from the design. Basically, the worker positions himself outside of the group boundary and manipulates the social variables in order to bring about desired changes in group behavior and/or individual member behavior. In some instances, such procedures can also influence the larger social system within which the group functions such as the hospital, the neighborhood, or the organization. The desired changes can be selected by the worker, or by the group; it does not matter to the design. The worker and/or the group can manipulate the variable; however, in the usual version of this design the worker is the crucial component. It is he who is the "change agent."

Social groupworkers recognize that program also can be used to alter positions, statuses, and roles of members and thereby influence individual behavior. Change could be achieved also through structuring the milieu. A simple illustration would be that of changing the room assignments of patients in a hospital. It is known that the relationships of those on the periphery differ from those in the center of a living complex, that closeness tends to produce affiliation, and that communication patterns will follow from location. Those patients nearest the nurses' station react differently from those at a distance. Studies indicate that the same factors operate in a housing complex.

The design as described here is not rejected in this book. What is rejected is its acceptance as a model for social work with groups because it deals with only one set of variables to the virtual exclusion of the needs of the individuals. This will be discussed later. In my opinion, this design is inappropriate for social work because it is not congruent with social work philosophy; it is not consistent with the knowledge base of social work; and it is ineffective for achieving social work objectives.

The student might assume at this point in the discussion that the broad field called group dynamics falls into this style. Basically, the group dynamics theorists use some of the concepts from the above formulation but they are more concerned with individual personality and its significance in the group and by the group. However, they still do not use the dynamics of personality and human relationships as the important dimensions even though it was Kurt Lewin, the father of group dynamics, who developed the formula that behavior is a function of the interaction of the person, his social situation, and the cultural context in which it takes place. The learning theorists, and recently the socio-behavioral advocates also, cannot be called social-variable interveners.

I wish to emphasize that the design which I am describing is not the true social-systems model. It is a popular orientation which one finds prevalent in groupwork. Its main characteristic is that it seeks to influence social variables which I call external because they are external to the individual, and it seems to rest upon the theory

14

that social variables are the major determinants
of individual behavior, to the exclusion of the
psychological attributes of the specific individuals. It also excludes the importance of the interaction between psychological and social variables.

A systems model accepts the fact that social
factors are determinants of human behavior but
holds that there are many other determinants. The
main distinction, however, is the interdependence
and interpenetration of many subsystems in interaction, and the influence they have on the whole
and on each other.

Learning Theory, Habit Formation, and Cognition

Another theoretical orientation that is becoming popular currently, although it is not new,
is the application of learning theory to social
work. Some of the groupwork theorists who espoused the social-variables approach described
above have switched recently to learning theory.

The group can be conceived of as an environment. Some theorists like to think of social
work with groups as social learning and teaching.
This is understandable as in the twenties much of
the literature in groupwork came out of the field
of progressive education. Max Siporin has written
that learning is the acquisition of new behavior
through experience in which the new behavior becomes habitual. "Socialization," he says, "is a
form of social learning through social experience."[1] The group is a powerful and viable medium
for such social learning. Lieberman, Laskin, and
Whitaker, discussing the characteristics of groups
which seem to have important influences on the
therapeutic experience of a patient suggest the
following:

1. The patient's feeling of belonging allows him to risk the disapproval of others (risk-

---

[1]Max Siporin, "Learning Theory: A Cautious
Approach to an Approach," (Baltimore: School of
Social Work, University of Maryland, October,
1968).

ing the disapproval of others is a fundamental
condition for the discovery of new patterns of behavior).

2. The group has the power to enforce the
norms and standards which the members set for themselves. It exerts great pressure to make the members conform and hence to make the patient change
his behavior or views. The power of members to
control behavior also implies that each member has
a greater opportunity to shape his environment in
a group than he has in individual therapy. A disregard for the rules of the group brings punishment.
In groups, punishment usually is either physical
or psychological exclusion. The group also offers
its rewards in terms of affirmation of both the
individual and his behavior.

3. The group has the capacity to define
reality for its members.

4. The group has the capacity to induce,
stimulate, and release powerful feelings. The individual may experience denied feelings in a corrective way, finding out that these feelings are
not as terrifying as he first thought.

5. The distribution of power and influence
is fluid in the group, whereas in individual psychotherapy the therapist has power over the situation. In groups, the therapist feels that he has
less responsibility for any individual and therefore he feels less relationship between his therapeutic intervention and behavior change.

6. The group has the capacity to provide a
context for social comparison and feedback. The
group allows the individual to understand better
the impact of his behavior on others.[1]

These six conditions provide a context for
learning in the group in the traditional sense of
learning. To some, learning means only behavior.
Learning also can apply to such things as self-
image, a sense of self-identity, self-worth, and

[1]Lieberman, Laskin, and Whitaker, "The Group
as a Unique Context for Therapy," Psychotherapy,
Vol. V, No. 1 (1951).

self-awareness, to name but a few. Siporin writes, "Behavior refers to response or activity on the part of an organism. Behavior is generally distinguished from response-activity in that it is structured, is observable, involves a sequence of responses, is largely habitual to the organism, and is learned....When learned, behavior and behavior systems become a behavior potential which is stored in the personality or the mind....Freud thought of behavior as unconsciously, pre-consciously, or consciously determined, but Skinner[1] considers all behavior to be overtly determined by reinforcement."

If all behavior is learned, or even if some is learned, then the group can be seen as a powerful and viable medium for learning new behaviors. Social work in the group is directed at enabling change from maladaptive behavior to adaptive behavior and to providing experiences through which coping behavior can be learned. To all intents and purposes, learning occurs through four means: by trial and error, by conditioning, through identification, and by cognition.

In the previous discussion of structural variables, the method of influencing change was said to be the manipulation of variables external to the individual; that is, group elements and group processes. In a cognitive or learning design, the worker focuses on external and internal variables. In one sense, the approach is to teach role expectations, role behaviors, norms, and skills or provide group experiences through which they can be learned. This involves role-taking, role playing, and role repetoires. In another sense, but not incompatible with the foregoing, the group experience provides a medium for habit training by stimulus, repetition, rewards, routines, and cognitive decision-making; that is, through the conscious choice of alternatives and options.

The design also provides the opportunity to emulate role models, be they the worker, peers, or fictional figures as in literature and drama.

---

[1]B. F. Skinner, Science and Human Behavior (New York: Macmillan Co., 1953).

This mechanism is a powerful one and can be a source of negative as well as positive learning. Sears discusses this in his work.[1] He also provides another dimension that explains, in part, learning through group experience.[2] He says that it is the environment which shapes behavior and suggests that the medium is the ongoing reduction of immediate needs as related to the prediction of subsequent behavior. Socially learned desires motivate behavior.

Sears contends that identification develops through the early experience of spontaneous imitation of behavior and is reinforced through recognition received for imitating behavior, and through the personal satisfaction of finding the behavior of others in one's own actions. Development is, then, a training process. Social behavior is said to depend almost exclusively upon the impact of others rather than upon any internal developmental processes. Genuine social learning depends upon replacing previous learning with newer experiences based upon more appropriate satisfactions rather than upon avoiding unpleasant experiences or upon fear of consequences.

In this design in groupwork, the relationship with the worker is crucial and the group must be a reference group; that is, the impact comes through significant others. The method which would follow from this formulation could be characterized as the application of training or management devices. Sears suggests that reasoning is less important than labeling. He suggests that it is a matter of explaining exactly what it is that one does or does not want the member to do. This is directing, and then sanctioning or rewarding the resulting behavior. Groupwork traditionally contains much of this kind of rationale and an examination of the earlier literature reveals that both leader-

---

[1]R. R. Sears, "Identification as a Form of Behavior Development in D. B. Harris," The Concept of Development (Minneapolis: University of Minnesota Press, 1957).

[2]Henry Maier, "The Learning Theory of Robert R. Sears," Three Theories of Child Development (rev., New York: Harper & Row, 1969), pp. 144-76.

ship and program were viewed in this manner.

Sears also speaks of reinforcement, but the work of Edwin J. Thomas spells out the use of such behavioral-science concepts in more detail.[1] Sheldon Rose has attempted to apply the theory to work with groups.[2] These formulations rest upon Skinner's research. The major ingredients in learning designs based upon Skinner's experiments consist of reinforcement (positive and negative), shaping, maintaining behavior, and extinction. The approach stresses the specific controlling variables in the person's environment that relate to the problematic behavior.

Thomas and Goodman say that they are not concerned with theories which hypothesize motivation. Such theories speculate about psychic processes which may or may not be related to environmental-change methods. However, they do allow that as socio-behavioral theory develops it may be supplemented with some theoretical orientations which do include human motivations.[3]

This book does not reject learning theory or socio-behavioral theory as applicable to social work with groups. It rejects any frame of reference which overemphasizes one aspect, be it social or psychological, to the neglect of the other and that fails to utilize an approach which includes the interaction and interpenetration of all pertinent systems while also taking into account the dynamics of transaction with the bounding systems.

It is accepted here that persons learn behavior and that the basic dynamics underlying social learning in the growing-up process rest

---

[1]E. J. Thomas and E. Goodman, _Socio-Behavioral Theory and Interpersonal Helping in Social Work_ (Ann Arbor: Campus Publishers, 1966).

[2]Sheldon Rose, "A Behavioral Approach to Group Treatment with Children," _The Socio-Behavioral Approach and Applications to Social Work_ (New York: Council on Social Work Education, 1969).

[3]Thomas and Goodman, _Socio-Behavioral Theory_, pp. 12-13.

upon reinforcement by significant others. There
is no doubt that behaviors are maintained and perpetuated by reinforcers. The group experience can
perpetuate certain behaviors; it can extinguish behaviors by ignoring or failing to reward, and it
can facilitate experimentation and shaping by support and the establishment of a free social climate.

It is not only possible but reasonable to direct these efforts to the specific variables which
are controlling in the person's environment that
apply to the problem behaviors. Group method in
the context of learning theory manipulates such
variables to effect desired outcomes. The manipulation may be directed by the worker, or may come
from the group, the latter may or may not be the
result of the worker's enabling. However, the
worker should not disregard differences among individuals, individual needs and predispositions, or
the goals of the individuals. With these limitations, the methodology is a viable one for treatment as well as development.

Ego Functioning, Coping, and Adaptation

Dynamic psychology and ego-psychology rely
heavily on individual or internal variables as
they interact with the environment. The variables
to be influenced, however, are the internal ones.
Ego-psychology has been espoused in social casework but groupwork has been slower to use it, continuing to rely upon sociology, social psychology,
and more lately, socio-behavioral concepts and
principles.

The group in social work may be viewed as a
milieu within which ego functioning may be strengthened through experiences which provide the opportunity for successful achievement in coping and
adaptation.[1] The central hypothesis is that individual behavior occurs as a result of the individual's ego responses to the processes of group
life. The member is obliged to change his way of
behaving as his usual modes of adaptation collide
with the requirements of the group structure and

---

[1]Marshall Edelson, Ego-Psychology, Group
Dynamics and the Therapeutic Community (New York:
Grune & Stratton, Inc., 1964).

its process problems. Through structured group
experiences, feedback, and awareness, and with
support in problem-solving, the member is enabled
to gain skills in coping and adaptation. The elements in this design are very similar to the familiar aspects of modern social work practice.
The group forms a here-and-now within which behavior can be examined, practiced, and adapted. The
group is a safe laboratory but it is also for real;
that is, the object relationships and problems of
living are within the members' life space. They
are not simulated nor are they secondhand. The
group provides events that have meaning for the
members in that the members do share a common destiny which derives from common interests and goals,
with developing common norms, and from common values. Moreover, the consequences of behavior are
meaningful because the interpersonal rewards and
sanctions (favorable or unfavorable responses) are
real.

Within this design, members can test reality
and compare their perceptions with those of others.
In this way they are able to gain a clearer perception of the outer world. At the same time and
in much the same way, members are able to perceive
more accurately and appraise themselves, their behaviors, and the resulting consequences; become
more knowledgeable about the drives which propel
them; and about their perceptions of social demands which come from internalized or conscious
norms and values. As a concomitant, often the
member also can learn about the reality of his
fears and the imagined consequences of his actions,
thoughts, and feelings. Cognitive processes are
exercised and distortions corrected, defenses are
illustrated and efforts supported to revise them
where appropriate and, as a result, object relationships can be tested, tried, and strengthened.
Program, as one example, provides a medium for
developing motor skills, thinking, and reeducat-
ing feelings.

One of the important aspects of ego growth
and function is the urge to alter the reality.
Through action to alter reality, it is possible
to repress unpleasant ideas. The urge or effort
is to master the environment or, at the least, to
deal effectively with the environment. More will
be said about this later, especially in regard to

social action as ego-building. Social action, as an end, has been part and parcel of social group-work and herewith it is suggested also as a means or as a part of the methodology.

This design provides the possibility for working through the conflict between wishes and fears by acting on wishes that have been suppressed and experiencing responses in a protected environmental setting that are not threatening or destroying. It also provides an opportunity for mutual support in person-to-person endeavors.

To be most effective, the group and its individuals should be guided into experiences that address themselves to the specific ego functions which require strengthening, and should be coupled with feedback that makes achievement known to the members. The method is predicated upon the assumption that the ego normally grows and develops as a result of experiences and forces that are identified and that ego functions can be assessed in the manner described. It is, then, a matter of consciously structuring experiences and manipulating those forces which allegedly produce ego strength.

Ego-Strengthening in the Eriksonian Frame of Reference[1]

The group in social work may be viewed as a developmental modality. The assumption is that ego develops through a gradual unfolding of the personality through phase-specific psychosocial crises; this is an epigenetic principle. This means that at each stage in the sequence there is a successive development of the parts of the personality. Each part existed before but it does not develop until the individual is ready through growth and maturation and until it is forced by pressures from society. The process is a continuous one so that every stage is related systematically to all other stages.

Each succeeding stage depends upon the suc-

---

[1]Erik H. Erikson, "Identity and the Life Cycle," Psychological Issues, Vol. I, No. 1, monograph 1 (1959).

cessful completion of the preceding stages, through the cycle to maturity. Failure to negotiate a stage results in specified ego defects. The stages bear repeating at this time. Trust versus mistrust (hope), autonomy versus shame and doubt (will), initiative versus guilt (purpose), industry versus inferiority (skill), identity versus identity diffusion (fidelity), intimacy versus isolation (love), generativity versus isolation (care), integration versus disgust and despair (wisdom).

The Eriksonian formulation lends itself very well to a design for groupwork, but this has not been developed in the literature. It is applicable both to a developmental group of normal individuals in group services agencies as well as to treatment groups.

Based upon an assessment of the stage of the psychosocial development of the group, one can decide the stance of the worker, the choice of program, and the kind of experience that is most appropriate. Also, one can use the stages conception as a guide for group composition and as a scale for evaluation. Erikson is very clear about the kind of caretaker and his stance (in this instance, the worker) that is preferred at each stage. He also implies the nature of the environmental setting. For example, persons with unresolved crises around autonomy will experience as endangering the typical authoritarian setting of some schools or institutions.

The formulation provides an excellent guide for the analysis and selection of program. To illustrate, crafts would seem to be appropriate for those in the industry phase, but competition would not be appropriate for the development of trust. Programs for adolescents might be built around experiences which foster identity, and so forth.

It would seem to be inadvisable to program for skill in the urban ghetto before basic trust has been negotiated. As a guide, the sequence would develop more appropriately around the hope that one can as a prerequisite to one's willing. If one can will, then this gives rise to the question "will what?" and, hence, to the motivation to seek for purpose. If one has a purpose, then and only then can the acquisition of needed skills to accomplish that purpose make sense. If one can have hope that one can, and will what one will, to do what one proposes, and one can acquire the skills which enable one to, one begins to know who and what one is.

It is an easy step from this point to devise programs which contain within them the elements that foster these virtues and give practice and exercise in them. While the Eriksonian frame of reference seeks to relate psychological tasks to societal demands, the main thrust seeks to identify the part played by the surrounding culture in individual growth. In a sense, one can alter the environmental influences in order to facilitate ego growth and strength. This formulation has much to offer for social work with groups.

There is some reason to believe that many emotional disturbances have their etiologies in specific stages of growth and development. Whether one relates them to classical Freudian stages, or to Eriksonian stages, or even to such theories as those which hold that deviant behavior is role enactment; the Eriksonian formulation can provide a guide for group composition and also for group-task orientations addressed to the stage-related emotional problem.

Garland, Jones, and Kolodny have developed a very interesting and useful application of this formulation to the stages of development of a group. Since it is not comparable to the designs being described here, it will not be explained further, but would be worth the reader's time to investigate.[1]

Socialization as a Means of Influencing Individual Behavior

Assumptions about socialization underlie much of the traditional social groupwork literature, up to as late as the nineteen fifties. It has been a premise that an objective of social groupwork has been to socialize the individual, and

---

[1]Garland, Jones, and Kolodny, "A Model for Stages of Development in Social Work Groups."

24

also that the group does socialize, and hence, inducts the individual into the culture.

Socialization and such concepts as the induction of persons into the prescriptions of the culture abound in sociology and social psychology. These ideas also have permeated groupwork thinking. The subject of socialization is too large to be dealt with here. It is important, however, to note that the introduction of a person into a culture has tribal overtones.[1] One is socialized into new or appropriate behavior through contagion, the force and effect of group pressure and social control, as well as the fear of sanctions. Such aspects as commitment, social rewards, and self-image enter into the behavioral determinants. Usually, membership in a group means accepting the group tenets, norms, values, and hence prescriptions.

The manner in which behavior is influenced may rest upon some of the other designs which have been discussed above, such as learning, or social-situational factors; but the group method here is a design for socialization. Some refer to it when discussing group culture; others imply its usefulness when considering the treatment stages in group development. In other words, the group is not considered a viable medium for treatment until it has coalesced sufficiently to have a group culture and, therefore, a socialization potential. The socialization design focuses on factors external to the individual.

Therapy, Personality, and Behavioral Change

It is meaningless to speak of a group therapy model since today there are many different definitions of therapy. Many writers regard therapy as a learning process and postulate that it requires the active interest and participation of the patient. This is said to be true regardless of how one regards the dynamics of cure, be it simple learning, enforcement, corrective experience, the result of insight, or the resolution of trans-

---

[1]Hans Toch, The Social Psychology of Social Movements (New York: Bobbs Merrill Co., Inc., 1965).

ference neuroses. Such a definition connotes a
melange of methodologies and, even so, it does not
take in the problem-solving, or the role-enactment
designs, nor does it embrace the game-theory therapies. Many of the so-called "moderns" would define therapy as a process which liberates one from
inhibiting fears, in a reliable, good relationship, and which frees the ego potential for creative self-realization and the birth of a real
self.

It was stated earlier in Section I that a
model is a way of stating a theory. It is an analogue of a theory built to solve a problem.
Since there are any number of theories about behavior and deviance, there are any number of so-
called group-therapy models. To list but a few:
(1) the conflict between wishes and fears is basic
to behavior and deviance; (2) the desire for closeness and the inability to achieve closeness; (3)
the conflict resulting from control and submission;
(4) hollowness at the center of the human being
called "ontological insecurity;" (5) crisis of
identity which is the empty center with its fear
of depersonalization; (6) the solution to having
to adapt to an insane society; (7) the result of
repression of normal instincts to conform to the
inhibiting demands of society; (8) the frustration in object relationships; (9) the double-bind
communication, and so on.

It does matter whether one is viewed as suffering from a social dysfunction or from an internal malfunction when selecting a treatment
modality. It matters also whether a person's behavior is thought of as predetermined or if he is
thought to be free to change if conditions change
or if he wishes to change. Group therapy designs,
therefore, should flow from the theories or assumptions about behavior which underlie each of
them.

In social work with groups, group treatment
is directed primarily at the conscious aspects of
behavior. It can be an ego-oriented design and
as such it tends to address itself to the internal
dynamics of the individual in transaction with the
environment or it can address itself to the group
variables, especially those of role, communication,
and awareness.

26

In technical parlance, there are two terms which refer to two types of adjustment: autoplasticism and alloplasticism. In the former type, man changes himself to fit his environment; in the latter, he changes the environment to make it respond to his desires. The psychotherapies are autoplastic, while the social approaches tend to be alloplastic. Both autoplastic and alloplastic adjustments have some value, but the exclusive pursuit of either exacts a price in terms of the other. It may be that too much emphasis on alloplastic adjustment exacts a high price in terms of autoplastic capabilities.

It is believed by some theorists that group treatment should be directed to the development of a maximum of adaptability in people. Others have argued that since reaction to frustration depends not only on the distance between desire and fulfillment, but also on the degree of frustration tolerance; group treatment should strengthen such tolerance.

Because there are many versions of group therapy and because many contain elements of the various designs discussed thus far, no attempt will be made to spell out the kinds and varieties. The usual designs one finds in social work address themselves to internal or psychic variables. They are either psychoanalytically based, including ego-psychology, or they take their theoretical base from social groupwork which traditionally has been closer to sociology and social psychology.

Inherent in a design that addresses itself to the internal factors are: (1) support, which is ego-restoring and ego-conserving, wherein the major techniques are suggestion, mobilization, manipulation, clarification, and interpretation; (2) awareness; (3) learning, including a reeducation of the ego.

Putting the concepts together in some general form, they include the following:

1. The group is viewed as a current reality; that is, as a slice of life, and hence behaviors within it and adaptations to it are genuine life experiences.

2. The group is a microcosm of the culture and, hence, the experience in the group is an engagement with reality-based demands, norms, and values.

3. The group is egalitarian and within it the resources are provided to all the members by all the members who participate as peers in a democratic community.

As of this writing, group therapy shows a movement away from treatment which is separated from life itself. The trend is to narrow the gap between practitioner and member, between life situations and treatment situations, and, hence, toward democracy in practice. This trend is in keeping with the current social movement which is tending to flatten out the differences between man and man, between worker and member, and attests to the power of peers.

The variables in the psychological-therapy design (generalizing from several) are past experiences which generate predispositions and defenses, and also are the determinants of self-concept, values, super-ego, wishes, anxieties, fears, and, hence, modes of behavior and adaptation. The wishes, anxieties, fears, defenses, and modes are generated from need dispositions which may or may not be linked to tissue needs (biological and physical). Such needs are related to motivations or drives.

The need dispositions include physical security, heterosexual satisfactions, expression of love, self-expression, orientation to one's place in society and the place of others, securing and maintaining membership in a definite human group, and a sense of belonging to a moral order and of being right in what one does.

Some of the dimensions of method in social work with groups in this context are the provision of an awareness of the inappropriateness of behavior, thought, feelings, attitudes, et cetera; an awareness of goals; feedback and confrontation; support; clarification; information-giving; interpretation; development of some insights; teaching; eliciting feeling; and so forth.

Within this context and in groupwork in general, there are other issues which determine method. These will be listed in order to fill out the options available in all of the designs discussed in this book. They are:

1. Permissive or structured approaches.

2. Discussion or activity.

3. Experiential or insightful approaches.

4. Worker-centered or group-process-centered approaches.

5. Approaches based upon the worker using prescribed objectives with selectively used techniques or the worker as a function and with a stance.

6. Historical and study-oriented or here-and-now, present-oriented approaches.

7. Approaches based upon the worker in a professional role confronting a person in a member role or a human confrontation between the two people who are engaged together in a cooperative enterprise.

Several Leading Designs in Social Groupwork

The term social groupwork used here means that specific area of concentration in social work so designated, as distinguished from the discussion in the last pages which included any form of social work which was conducted with groups. The previous discussion was more general in its attempt to describe various designs for working with groups. The discussion to follow is specific to social groupwork which is more narrowly defined.

There are several leading writers in social groupwork whose work needs to be mentioned in any discussion of groupwork designs. They do not present their orientations in the format used in this book, and, hence, their presentations overlap the categories used in this book. Rather than presenting Robert Vinter and William Schwartz, an excerpt from Emanuel Tropp will be introduced with a mini-

29

mum of supplementary comment.[1]

"Today in the arena of social group work theory
there are two polar views, and various people take
stands at stages in between. There is Robert Vinter
at one end, who sees the group as a means by which
the worker can meet individual treatment goals--
carefully studied and diagnosed, and prescribed
for each member in the group--by unashamedly manipulating the group and its members to achieve these
highly particularistic and differentiated goals.[2]
In 1959, Vinter honestly faced a dilemma that he
was unable to resolve: If the natural forces of
group life are the most potent means of effecting
individual change in the group, how can the worker
justify becoming deeply involved in controlling
and fragmenting the group process."[3] The dilemma
Tropp speaks of seems to have been resolved in
favor of the worker being the change agent.
Vinter's orientation has been related to social
psychology in the past, and today, the Michigan
School is moving closer to a socio-behavioral base.

Tropp continues, "At the other pole is William
Schwartz[4] who has developed the concept of the
group as a system of mutual aid and who sees the
group and its living experiences as the crucial
focus of the worker. He sees the worker and the

---

[1]Emanuel Tropp, "The Group: In Life and in
Social Work," Social Casework (May, 1968), 267-74.

[2]Robert D. Vinter, ed., Readings in Group
Work Practice (Ann Arbor: Campus Publishers,
1967).

[3]Robert D. Vinter, "Small Group Theory and
Research: Implications for Group Work Practice
Theory and Research," Social Science Theory and
Social Work Research, Kogan, ed. (National Assoc-
iation of Social Work, 1960).

[4]William Schwartz, "The Social Worker in the
Group," Social Welfare Forum (New York: Columbia
University Press, 1961), pp. 159-72.

Also Lawrence Shulman, Casebook in Social Work
with Groups (New York: Council on Social Work
Education, 1968).

members as engaged in a common enterprise, that of carrying on the group's purpose. He sees the individual members as growing essentially through their group-oriented efforts. Now, Schwartz's position vis-à-vis Vinter's, holds within it something far more important than a technical difference. It is a philosophical difference--the value orientation--that is strikingly at issue. To Schwartz, the group is not a melange of wholes and parts to be arranged, taken apart, put back together, and generally manipulated by a social worker in accordance with his own goals for different individuals; to him, the group is an organic whole that develops a life of its own and an integrity of its own, which the worker had better respect if he is to be useful."[1]

The Schwartz design views the group process as the important influence for growth and change. The major theme centers around mutual aid. The most recent statements by Schwartz and his adherents go beyond mutual aid of member to member and suggest that the assignment is to mediate. By this is meant that the person and his society reach out for each other as they have a mutual need for self-fulfillment and the worker mediates this process.

The mediation in Schwartz's terms consists of searching out the common ground between the client's perception of his own need and the aspects of social demand with which he is faced; detecting and challenging the obstacles; contributing data, facts, and value concepts; lending a vision; and defining the requirements and limits of the situation in which the client-worker system is set.

Schwartz disagrees with those who hold that the acts of the worker can be consciously performed, based upon analysis of the process at that moment or upon individual diagnoses. His emphasis is in developing the tasks on broad categories of actions such as sets. One also gathers from his writing that understanding the group member is not based upon the usual notions of psychological functioning but upon comprehending his behavior within

---

[1]Tropp, "The Group: In Life and in Social Work."

systems. This seems to imply that behavior can be assessed as appropriate or inappropriate; that is, functional or nonfunctional within the system, and also within the value orientation of the system, instead of upon some internal set of psychic norms. He is concerned with what the member does and not what he is.

One senses in Schwartz some of Parson's thinking, some of Thomas Szasz, and a little existentialism. The central assumption rests upon an interdependence between the individual and society. This book is in agreement with this assumption. The design, however, does not spell out the variables that are significant in this interdependence and, hence, the mediation involves more art than science, and more "happening" than goal facilitation. The worker here seems to be skilled in procedure rather than in content which is also in agreement with the thesis of this book. Schwartz's contribution to the practice of social work has been most valuable. It allows the worker wide latitudes of style, but in actual practice, it is difficult to predict outcomes, and it is very hard to evaluate the effectiveness of the method. This may not be a criticism or an objection. The design fits very comfortably into the social philosophy of the times; namely, reduction of authoritarian control, egalitarianism or partnership of the worker and client, equality of peers in a mutual-aid endeavor, and the importance of using systems concepts to analyze social phenomena. The Schwartz formulation, while designed for social groupwork, is applicable to social work generally.

Tropp has been endeavoring to conceptualize social groupwork practice himself. He believes that groupwork is the principal social work practice suited and equipped to work with people with average functioning. He holds that for such people, that is, the normal and average, in order to achieve optimum social functioning, group experiences must be challenging, demanding, and externally-oriented rather than protected, permissive, or self-oriented. He believes that group members should be afforded a wide variety of social experiences approximating those of society.

Tropp says that the real business of groupwork is the testing of members against the demands of organized society. This testing he describes as the acting out of the drama of the individual against, through, and for society. This point of view differs from Schwartz's who sees the worker as mediating between the individual and society.

Tropp sees social groupwork only in terms of goal-oriented groups which he says are common-goal groups. In such groups, members should not be involved primarily with their individual needs. The core of his thesis is that group-goal achievement is the primary dynamic in the social growth of the members. It follows then that "effective achievement" and "responsible engagement" are the primary focii of the groupworker. In essence, Tropp is interested in the social growth of the group members.[1]

Tropp does not believe that social groupwork is applicable to treatment or therapy groups. The position in this book is that Tropp's stance is defensible by definition only. Social work in groups is method and is applicable and viable for a variety of purposes, including treatment. This position will be discussed further in other parts of the book.

More recently, Tropp seems to have changed his focus somewhat and now assumes an existential position.[2] In a recent paper he suggests that the worker need have no particularized or differentiated knowledge of each individual in the group and decries the use of diagnosis in groupwork. He confirms the idea that it is the group that is the helping agent and deprecates the study-diagnosis-treatment approach in social groupwork. The main thrust of the paper is that of a human confrontation in which the member is not a client but a

---

[1]Emanuel Tropp, "Group Intent and Group Structure: Essential Criteria for Group Work Practice," Journal of Jewish Communal Service (Spring, 1965), 239-50.

[2]Emanuel Tropp, "A Humanistic View of Social Group Work: Worker and Member on a Common Human Level," paper delivered at 95th Annual Forum of the National Conference of Social Work (May 29, 1968).

human being in interaction with other human beings in the group. In the design, the _group_ (not the individuals) is the unit requiring assessment, planning, and evaluation within what Tropp calls a humanistic view of the worker function.

In one way, the idea of the group being the unit requiring assessment, planning, and evaluation falls into a systems approach within which the relationships (structure) of the group are the focus. In another way, the group is a system of mutual aid. It is not clear just what variables Tropp considers significant for the endeavor.

The Existential Component in Social Work

To understand Tropp's position, and to be aware of some of the themes which are undertones in the work of Schwartz and Shulman, it seems useful to examine briefly some dimensions of existentialism.

One of the most significant aspects has been mentioned in discussing Tropp's work; namely, that the encounter in social work must occur between person and person rather than between role and role. Sinsheimer speaks of the consultation in therapy as being an experience involving genuine self-disclosure. The client opens himself as a — patient and the social worker opens himself as a person. It is the hope that both will grow in the encounter if each can be free to be himself. In such a relationship, Sinsheimer holds, each divests himself of his masks and can experience the thrill of feeling safe enough to risk an open confrontation with another person. From such confrontation, it is alleged, can come greater strength with which to cope with one's problems and sorrows.[1] One might substitute "group experience" for consultation and see confrontation of peer to peer and member to worker as the encounter. Then, worker and member are equals, albeit with differing functions and contributions in the group.

A second important aspect is in the invoca-

---

[1]Robert Sinsheimer, "The Existential Case Work Relationship," _Social Casework_ (February, 1969), 67-73.

tion of love. Of this Sinsheimer says that the worker must free himself from preconceived formulations and diagnostic labels. The client must be perceived as a person and not as an object derived from abstract formulations. The most important element is love and it is this that differentiates existential treatment from other forms of therapeutic relationships. Love, of course, means caring and being concerned. It is essential in this frame of reference that the treatment be within the context of an experience in self-disclosure, love, communion, and an active coming together.

Concepts such as love[1] make it difficult if not impossible to apply a rigorous approach to the helping process. Love is hard to quantify and to feed into a computer. The exponents of existentialism contend that not all of living or of the world can be demonstrated by scientific method, nor can all aspects of human relationships or behavior be understood and explained by formulae, nor can they be quantified. The scientists, and especially the behavioral scientists, seem to respond by alleging that if it cannot be fed into a computer it does not exist, or they deny it, or they ignore it.

Another aspect of existential thinking lies in the idea that one cannot predict the outcome of a sequence of human interactions because emergent consequences evolve. Such a notion precludes interventions into the group process to effect known or even predictable outcomes. Things happen and conduct themselves to ends and it is in the happening that growth can eventuate. These notions also lead to the conclusion that setting objectives in advance automatically limits the possible creative results. One cannot know what might develop in truly creative style because creating should mean going beyond the limits of what is known.

Krill has been foremost in endeavoring to introduce existential thinking into social work. In two articles he explores the possible applications

---

[1]Also hate, anxiety, etc.

of these ideas in social practice.[1] The ideas he
develops concern themselves with freedom, manipulation, choice, responsibility, closeness, commitment, and self-actualization. These kinds of
words are anathema to the researcher and, hence,
create very real problems in empirical studies.
Existentialism refers to the term existence to
mean man's possibility of being himself by realiz-
ing his potentials to the full. This idea has
been in the social groupwork literature since that
literature first began to appear. This school of
thought is concerned essentially with the issues
of human freedom, choice, and responsibility. One
holds that man is a free agent who achieves meaning through choice within options. It concerns
itself also with pain and suffering as inevitable
in the human condition.

To view the group experience in existential
terms means that one cannot find man while seeking
underlying causal relationships in behavior or in
a deterministic view. There are several very important postulates: Man has the potential freedom
to make choices in a responsible manner though
that freedom may be impaired by inner conflicts,
blockages in development, or external forces; man
can find meaning in life through liberation of his
inner strengths; dignity is inherent in the human
condition; and man is in the process of becoming.
And so, it has been said that the presence of love
is the only healer.

Krill requires self-encounter in the treatment process. He identifies Mower and Glasser as
stating that the key factor in therapy is helping
a patient to identify clearly for himself how he
believes he ought to behave and what values seem
important to him personally. He can then identify
how his actual decisions and behavior are at odds
with the way he wants to be. The necessity of
changed behavior is stressed, regardless of feelings involved, in order to bring about the person's

---

[1]Donald F. Krill, "Existentialism: A Philosophy for our Current Revolutions," Social Service
Review (September, 1966), 289-301.

Also, "Existential Psychotherapy and the problem
of Anomie," Social Work (April, 1969), 33-49.

acceptance of himself as worthy and hence acceptable to others.

Krill suggests, however, that individuals are manipulated by others and that manipulation shuts out the potential for growth and destroys the freedom of a relationship.[1] He argues that the worker should confront the individual with a sense of his own freedom. The therapy lets the client know his life is not predetermined, but that he has an active choice in his life and how he will live it; choice is made in the present, and if it is not predetermined, then the historical study is not relevant. The encounter is in the here-and-now and needs to be understood only in that context. If past causal relationships are denied, then it is the present that matters.

The group member must realize the necessity for dialogue without manipulation hindering his freedom. Closeness and personal growth are interrelated, and without closeness to another being growth is impaired. In order to achieve closeness, trust must be established and the client must accept a way of commitment. Krill emphasizes too that the individual also must be concerned with what goes on outside of him. Potentialities must be drawn upon in life.

Admittedly, this is philosophy, but Martin Rein has written, "The more ruthlessly we pursue the path of technology the more we come to acknowledge the role of ideology in the selection among policy alternatives."[2]

In these ideas one finds similarities to, if not the foundations for, some of Schwartz's and Tropp's writings about social groupwork. Schwartz alleges that both individual diagnosis and treatment goals impede the growth that potentially can come through process. Schwartz wants to neutralize the control over the person so that he can be free to become. One senses also that interper-

---

[1]Krill, "Existentialism: A Philosophy for our Current Revolutions."

[2]Martin Rein, <u>American Institute of Planners Journal</u> (May, 1967), 162.

sonal convergence based upon human acceptance of
one another is a crucial component of his method.
Essentially, while Schwartz mediates, he also
frees the member to grow. Tropp is most emphatic
in his rejection of individual diagnosis, and of
history-taking. He posits the experience in the
here-and-now, and also stresses the human confrontation inherent in disclosure, trust, and egalitarianism. In these contributions to groupwork,
feelings are considered to be important. The approaches are not small-group-theory oriented, nor
do they rely on manipulating external variables.
They are not predeterministic either and cannot be
classified as psychoanalytical, nor are they essentially cognitive. They are not based upon
learning theory such as reinforcement or conditioning. They are, however, important contributions
to the development of a model for social work with
groups.

Social Goals and Social Action

The development of social groupwork in social
work has been coupled with social action since its
earliest writings. Clara Kaiser, Grace Coyle,
Dorothea Spellman, Gertrude Wilson, Alan F. Klein,
Wilber Newstetter, and others, to mention but a
few, included social action and social goals in
their definitions of social groupwork.

Coyle spoke of developing social responsibility and active citizenship for the improvement
of a democratic society. In "Group Work and Social
Change," a paper given at the National Conference
of Social Work in Montreal in 1935, she said, "It
(groupwork) cannot avoid also social responsibility
for the making of citizens--that is, for the production in individuals of those attitudes and ac-
complishments which will contribute to the kind of
society we desire." She elaborated by speaking of
four emphases in groupwork, one of which is "emphasis reflecting attitudes toward citizenship and
community participation resulting in education and
action on social questions...."[1]

------

[1]Grace Coyle, "Hast any Philosophy in Thee
Shepherd?" Group Experience and Democratic Values
(New York: Woman's Press, 1947), p. 170.

Gertrude Wilson, summarizing the field in 1943 said, "It (groupwork) is a process through which group life is influenced by a worker who consciously directs the interacting process toward the accomplishment of a social goal concerned in a democratic philosophy."[1] In this article she devoted a section to "Group Work and Social Action," confirming the relationship of these two endeavors.

Konopka finds that there is a dichotomy here because, on the one hand, she believes that the member in the growth-oriented group needs direct help with his problems and his personal development, whereas the member in the social-action group needs help in being effective on behalf of solving the problems that do not lie within himself or in his relationship with others.[2] This is undoubtedly true, but Coyle, Kaiser, Klein, and others hold that an indispensable part of individual growth and development is learning to be a citizen and also taking responsibility for social change toward socially desirable goals.

In 1964, Klein, Meyerson, Rubenstein, and Sirls set forth a reaffirmation of the social action component being indispensable in social groupwork in what has been called the Pittsburgh position.[3] They contend that there is a unity between social action and individual psychological health and ego strength. This position rests, in part, upon the assumption that it is debilitating to feel that one has no power to influence one's environment and that the result of such a feeling of being helpless and manipulated leads to apathy and a sense of worthlessness and inadequacy. Some would say that the effect is infantilizing and

---

[1]Gertrude Wilson, Social Work Year Book, 1943 (New York: Russell Sage Foundation), pp.494-98.

[2]Gisela Konopka, Social Group Work: A Helping Process (Englewood Cliffs, N. J.: Prentice-Hall, Inc., 1963).

[3]Alan F. Klein et al, "Social Group Work Practice Elaborated: A Statement of Position," (Pittsburgh: University of Pittsburgh, Graduate School of Social Work, April, 1964).

leads to dependency; others would argue that it can lead also to hostility and anger which could be internalized and directed at one's self or to acting out against others.

The lack of power to affect the environment is likened to the early crisis of autonomy wherein the toddler feels that he has not attained control over his own body and its functions and suffers a sense of doubt and shame. The point of view has been explained by Goffman who has written that total institutions take away or corrupt those things which in civil society give a person some sense of power over his world. They destroy his sense of autonomy and undermine his sense of self-determination. He is divested of any feeling of freedom of action. Goffman contends that a failure to retain autonomy or the competency to act in an adult, executive capacity produces a sense of terror in an inmate who is, in a real sense, infantilized.[1] Goffman overstates the case for the civil society. There are many adults and many more children in society who find themselves at the mercy of forces over which they have no control and whose reactions are comparable, therefore, to the institution patients whom Goffman describes.

The social groupwork writers predicated their adherence to social action and social goals on a philosophical stance and on the desirability of educating persons for citizenship in a democracy. There were two focii elaborated in the literature. One took the line that groups were important instruments through which to effect social change and, hence, social workers helped to develop strong, functioning groups to achieve these ends. The other held that group experience was a training in group life through which individuals could learn how to effect social change through democratic means and also develop an attitude and commitment to social change for the good of society and its citizens.

Grace Coyle strongly believed that the social

---

[1] Erving Goffman, _Asylums, Essays on the Social Situations of Mental Patients and other Inmates_ (Garden City, N.Y.: Anchor Books, Doubleday & Co., Inc., 1961), p. 43.

nature of man grows to its fullest only when he
uses himself with and for the benefit of others.
It is through his ability to have mutual relations
with others that he is socialized. To be mature,
she felt, one has to be able to identify one's
self with the good of the social whole as one sees
it and seek ends beyond self-interest. To discover
and commit one's self to one's social objects, in
her view, is as important to fulfillment as to
find the objects of personal loves.[1] Here Coyle
alluded to the importance of social action to the
individual actor in addition to the importance of
the goal for society or the common good. Although
Konopka presents a dichotomy as late as 1963,[2] it
seems preferable to avoid such discreteness and
to postulate that social action is important in
ego development and also that work with groups does
have a potential for teaching skills in a partic-
ipatory democracy and for achieving social change.

Robert W. White believes that the feeling of
efficacy is a primary, biological endowment and
it inheres in dealing effectively with the environment. He indicates that one aspect of reality in
ego terms is the endeavor to make a real alteration in external circumstances. Although his examples are derived from observing infants and
small children, his arguments seem reasonable in
thinking about older children and adults. He sees
as a primary ego task that of mastering the environment. Competence, in White's terms, comes
from cumulative learning as one learns to become
effective in dealing with surroundings through action. Efficacy is central to the adaptive process. Competence is the existing capacity to interact effectively with the environment.[3]

Competence, then, is a cumulative result of

---

[1]Grace Coyle, Group Work with American Youth
(New York: Harper & Brothers, 1948).

[2]Konopka, Social Group Work: A Helping
Process.

[3]Robert W. White, "Ego and Reality in Psychoanalytic Theory," Psychological Issues, Vol. III,
monograph 11 (New York: International Universities Press, 1963).

one's whole history of transactions with the environment. Self-respect and security rest upon the feeling of social competence.[1] Self-esteem springs from what one can make the environment do as well as the feedback from others because of what the person has done.

Of special interest here is White's observation that efficacy is activity that is not motivated by physical need, but by the satisfaction in the doing. There is an intrinsic striving which tends to produce gains which can be seen clearly only during those spare-time activities when body-cravings are in abeyance. These ideas have applicability to work with groups because they give rationale for transactions and for social action in practice, especially as they relate to self-image, interpersonal relations, ego function, and social learning within groups in social work.

White holds that we gain the knowledge of the probable consequences of action from our experiences with the environment. Our experience with the environment teaches us what we are able to do, what we might be able to do, as well as what we cannot do and probably cannot do. It is through such knowledge of the realities that we develop and channel our instinctual energies and learn to act within realistic limitations and facilitations.[2]

Social action need not connote a march on Washington, nor major legislative action. I have pointed out elsewhere that social action as discussed here can mean also social change in the agency, in the group itself, and in the changed values or behaviors of others.[3] In large or small action, the cumulative learning discussed by White can be effected.

Hyman J. Weiner argues that groupwork should adopt a view which seeks to combine both the

---

[1] Ibid., p. 41.

[2] Ibid., pp. 69-70.

[3] Alan F. Klein, Society, Democracy, and the Group (New York: Whiteside, Inc., 1953).

psychological and social dimensions of human existence. He asks for a "cultivation of social consciousness in groups elevated to the same priority as the goal of developing closer interpersonal relations."[1]

In the earlier theoretical writings, social action was espoused as philosophy or policy. This book reaffirms the purpose and the philosophy of social work as requiring social change. There is also recent agreement that the question is more than a philosophical one. The environment must be enhancing, and its dangers neutralized if man is to achieve his potential within it. Much behavior is malfunctional because of the lack of social nutrients in the environment, because of the frustrations and double-binds, and also the noxious elements which insult the biological and psychological functioning of the individual. Powerlessness, frustration, deprivation, and abuse not only can stunt growth, they also can make people sick.[2] The social group can be a potent force for change, and also a viable teaching ground for the learning of the skills needed to bring about change. The group is also an environment for its members and as such is a life space for developing a feeling of efficacy, achieving competence, and for reality experience in coping or matching the needs of individuals and societal needs by changes in either or both.

[1]Hyman J. Weiner, "Social Change and Social Group Work Practice," Journal of Social Work, Vol. IX, No. 3 (July, 1964), 106-12.

[2]Alexander Leighton et al, My Name Is Legion (New York: Basic Books, Inc., 1959).

CHAPTER 2

SEVERAL IMPORTANT CONCEPTS IN GROUPWORK

Purpose

The purpose for which a group is organized is a primary determinant of the choice of methodology. The lack of clarity about this has resulted in confusion. Such confusion seems to abound in small group research wherein conclusions are attributed to "groups" as though all human groups were alike and, therefore, findings with one kind of group can be attributed to all groups.[1] Also, there are contradictions in the social work literature wherein growth-oriented groups are distinguished from task-oriented groups on the one hand, with groupwork said to be usable only with one or the other, while on the other hand, some authorities contend that groupwork is applicable to all kinds of groups. For example, Tropp sees the goal-oriented group as the only group in which one practices social groupwork.

Tropp, however, is one of the few who discusses purpose as a determinant of method in any detail. He says, "...but there are distinct and crucially important differences in basic group approaches that must be understood in order to know when to use which approach and when not to, and when one may blend approaches and when this is not feasible. To achieve such an understanding, one must look at the group's purpose, function, and structure.

"The purpose of a group--why it is formed-- is the principle element to be defined....If the group leader has not thought clearly about purpose, he will find himself drifting with the group into irrelevant, unproductive, and meaningless areas, into confusing situations and shaky operational patterns."[2]

---

[1]Alan F. Klein, "Not All Groups Are Groups," Food for Thought (Toronto: Canadian Association for Adult Education, May, 1957).

[2]Tropp, "The Group: In Life and in Social Work."

This book postulates purpose as an indispensable element in any discussion of work with a group. The social agency, hospital, organization, or other sponsor, must know why it wants to use a group before a group is chosen as a strategy of choice. Purpose acts as a guide in determining group size. The larger the group, from about five on, the less viable it will be in enhancing behavior determinants such as self-image, value orientations, and coping mechanisms.

Purpose guides composition. One chooses members and arranges composition to a large extent based upon purpose.[1] Purpose is important in grouping in the practice of social work. Writers who give blanket prescriptions for grouping such as demographic data, problem homogeneity, degree of remission, and so on are failing to recognize that group purpose may affect group process and, hence, is crucial in relation to outcomes. Decision-making groups, such as those involved in social planning, are more likely to be influenced by heterogeneity of education, language, age, and so forth than a group of persons who are hurting inside because they have sick children. One composes an educational group differently from a treatment group. There is no intent here to list purposes and differences but only to illustrate that the consideration of the purpose is a sine qua non.

Structure flows from purpose. A diagnostic group should have a minimum of structure because structure organizes relationships and standardizes norms. The lack of structure makes it more likely that people will behave as they usually do and be themselves. Also, the lack of structure creates anxiety. The worker will be able to see defenses and modes of adaptation more readily than he would with structure. If purpose is goal directed, structure appropriate to the task should evolve. In a similar way, once purpose is clear, the group members can know what they are to do in order to carry out the purpose. This is called function. Structure and function flow from purpose.

---

[1]William Shalinsky, "Group Composition as an Element of Social Group Work Practice," Social Service Review, Vol. XLIII, No. 1 (March, 1969), 42-49.

Method can be reviewed on a continuum, and hence, it can be argued that there is one method with much variety of emphases. However, there are a great many variables that can be influenced when working with a group. The choice of which variables are significant must be related to the purpose for which the group has been organized. Change in some is more likely to produce the desired end than change in others. Some may be more easily influenced or may be more accessible.

In a systems approach, variables within the individual member may be selected; or in his life space such as family; or in the group itself; or in the environment of the group, such as the agency, the neighborhood, a larger unit; or even in the recipient of the group's output. For any one system, the larger system to which it belongs is its environment, and the smaller systems within it are its components. Any influence of the environment on a given system is an input to the system, and any influence of the system on its environment is an output. Purpose must influence the choice of the group's and the worker's methods, whether it be to change individuals, systems, society, or any combination of them.

In summary, groups are not alike. In social work, groups differ as to the purpose for which they are formed. This difference matters a great deal as to how one composes them, how they are structured, what variables are significant, where one directs the impact of method, and what methods one uses.

Work with groups in social work is applicable to a wide variety of group purposes ranging through development, treatment, rehabilitation, correction, and social change. There are a variety of modes which comprise group method.[1] The battery of available modes within a social work frame of reference gives the worker options which provide a differential approach in groupwork. The selection of modes depends upon a conscious choice related

---

[1]Mode is being used here to inform that "group method" is, in fact, made up of many methods. Mode means a manner of doing something or performing a particular function or activity.

to purpose and to the assessment of what variables are significant, where the impact will provide maximum growth for minimum effort, and what is accessible within the setting and situation.

Social groupwork is not by any standard a unified, bounded, and well-defined entity. There are many different interpretations of what social groupwork is. It is hardly defensible to contend that social groupwork is applicable only to goal-oriented groups, so-called treatment groups, or to any one kind of group. As of this writing, social groupwork is a method in social work. The word "method" is used in a collective sense to mean an orderly procedure or process, a regular way or manner of doing something. It is characterized by regularity or habitual practice in action. Social groupwork is such a method, composed of a large variety of modes or specifics, from which a worker selects that which is appropriate and effective for the purposes desired within the social work context.

Differentiation for the purpose of exclusion or boundary seems to be less than useful at this time when the major concern should be effectiveness in serving members and the society within which social work operates. The effort to preserve social groupwork as a narrowly-defined entity is not in the best interest of the profession. Social work is working with individuals, groups, communities, organizations, and the like for social work purposes within a social work value system. What a social worker can help group members achieve through group process is the focus of this book. Whether one calls it social groupwork, or social work in groups, as long as it is social work and it operates through the focus on group process, the theoretical orientation which is presented in Section II is applicable.

This book also contends strongly that social work with groups, as discussed herein, is not only applicable to the so-called traditional group services agency but is essential to it. Purpose guides the selection of methodological options, and hence, the purposes subsumed under developmental groups, ideological groups, or goal-oriented groups provide the opportunity to utilize group methods effectively in the group services field.

Admittedly, this is a statement of opinion, philosophy, and definition. Can it be defended? There is no logic in what is considered a field of practice in social work today and the classification of methods by the number of clients being served is equally illogical. The present division into casework, groupwork, and community work, exists because of historical factors of various kinds. Vinter has said that the only real differences in these designations is the number of persons being served. A more useful distinction for the classification of practice might be purpose as related to that which one seeks to effect. The curriculum study states, "By social group work method is meant the systematic ways in which the worker affects social and group processes to achieve specified objectives."[1]

In 1963, the National Association of Social Workers Practice Statement said, "He (the group worker) uses his method toward the restoration of personal and social dysfunctioning and the prevention of social and personal breakdown, but also toward the promotion of normal social growth, especially in stress periods, and to provide for personal enhancement and to develop citizen participation. In these three latter purposes, social group work may differ in some degree from other methods of social work practice." In 1963, when this statement was published, social work was already started on the way toward a "combined methods orientation." In 1969, many schools of social work are offering an integrated approach to methods as the practice sequence. This does not mean one unified method, but that the practitioner has a repetoire of social work methods from which to choose, depending upon purpose, setting, strategy, target, and who the client is considered to be. This trend was inevitable since the behavioral sciences were moving in the direction of viewing behavior as a function of individual, group, and societal factors and because of the growing acceptance of a systems frame of reference.[2]

---

[1]Council on Social Work Education, Vol. XI, 1959, p. 31.

[2]The term "generic" can apply only to abstract propositions. On an operational level there are different methods on a continuum predicated on differences in clientele, purpose, and setting.

Social organization is not the same as physiological or mechanical organization. Groups and intergroups are involved in complex psychic interactions which include many aspects of systems processes. The individual is truly social and the group is truly psychical. Groups and individuals are not discrete. The behaving individual, the psychological person, is essentially an organization that is developed and maintained through continual, ongoing, symbolic interchange with other persons.[1] Esteem and prestige, authority and power, expertise and leadership, ego strength and competence underlie group decisions and these, in turn, channel actions, attitudes, collective behavior, and social change.[2] The individual, the group, and the community constitute open systems which interchange input and output constantly.

The variables which are significant for influence and change by the social worker differ from system to system and in relation to the proximate purposes and desired outcomes. All of the fields or methods in social work have similar ultimate goals. The proximate goals determine the significant variables to be influenced, allegedly to bring about change in a given subsystem and thus, in turn, help to determine the means. Group methods may be the appropriate means for achieving certain outcomes in any field of social work practice and can be utilized by a social worker. It seems obvious that group methods are applicable in treatment and also in goal-oriented groups. As long as the ways used by the worker affect group process to achieve the specified objectives, currently, one calls this groupwork. Does it matter whether one calls it social groupwork, social work in groups, or social work? If a person who is called a caseworker is utilizing the group experience as a social worker, the premises set forth in this book apply. Social groupwork is not defined as that which a social groupworker does; nor is it defined by the fields of practice or the setting. A social worker today operates with an armamen-

---

[1]Walter Buckley, Sociology and Modern Systems Theory (Englewood Cliffs, N. J.: Prentice-Hall, Inc., 1967), p. 44.

[2]Ibid., p. 129.

tarium of methods and part of his skill is in knowing which one to use when. The acceptance of a systems approach seems to lead one to the conclusion that a variety of methods must be employed simultaneously or in tandem in order to facilitate a "matching"[1] of individual and environment. "I suggest simply that the social approach or strategy by whatever method or means in approaching the person-in-situation complex is to achieve a <u>matching</u> of significant elements in coping patterns and environmental qualities in order to improve the consequences for both the individual and his environment."[2] Such matching implies changes in either or both, but most likely in both.

Contract

Contract is a term used infrequently in social groupwork, but it does appear in the writings of some authors. The concept is frequently employed in the group therapies. It is presented here as an important aspect of group method in the context of this book.

Contract is the agreement, usually verbal and nonverbal, between the worker and the group members and among themselves about the purpose of the group endeavor. The hypothesis is that if members do not know for what they are there, it is unlikely that they will be able to work to achieve the purpose, or be able to work together, or appropriately. The contract mobilizes and focuses the group energies. It is the premise that the group process is the change or growth-producing medium. For the group to move toward desired outcomes, the group members must be aware of what they are working on and toward.

Even if one argues that outcomes cannot be predicted in a system, or that they ought not to be predicted because the value lies in the crea-

---

[1]This word is used by William Gordon in "Constructs for Organizing Social Work Knowledge," a working paper for the Subcommittee on Knowledge-Building, National Association of Social Workers, Commission on Practice, October, 1966.

[2]Ibid.

tive happening, one can agree that the purpose is growth, or an experience, or the freeing of creative potentials.

Contract also is an agreement about expectations of the reciprocal roles of the worker, the members, and the sanctioning agency. Clarity about reciprocal-role expectations is important because it forestalls disappointments, frustrations, uncertainties, and also it gives some direction to what participants can work at and how. Like all contracts, it is negotiated by the participants and provides the framework, opportunities, and limits of the human encounters to follow. The contract is not immutable; it can be changed by the participants by negotiation when appropriate and as the need or desire arises.

The setting of a contract insures the democratic rights of the members, emphasizes the egalitarian quality of the enterprise and, hopefully, minimizes control and manipulation. It is also an essential in the establishment of morale since morale presupposes acceptance of group goals.

Let us hope that it is possible to clarify the semantics. Once a growth-oriented group sets a contract there is a goal. Likewise, the contract in a treatment group establishes a goal or goals such as, "we are here to get well," or "we are here to help each other get well," or even "we are here to know and reveal ourselves." A dichotomy between goal achievement and treatment is false once there is understanding that in a treatment group wherein group methods are used, the group not the worker is the therapeutic agent and the group is actively engaged in problem-solving and goal achievement.

Let us look beyond treatment to the goal of social change. This book cannot accept the traditional approach wherein it is assumed that individual growth and social change are outcomes of two discrete methods that must be kept separate, or that one can either enhance individual functioning or manipulate social variables in discrete compartments. Change methods are on a continuum, and individual and social variables are in constant interaction through feedback loops.

One of the keys to understanding such a con-

struct is the concept of linkage. Linkage concerns itself with the articulation of two or more
systems. It becomes necessary, if there is to be
progress in social work service to clients, to
discard anachronistic titles and dichotomies.
Modern systems analysis is built upon a dynamic
feedback model which does not allow one to think
of narrow boundaries, because change in any part
of a system presupposes change in other parts, and
in social systems one must always be conscious
that human beings make choices from a range of
options and, hence, one cannot (or should not) disregard the human component in the social-change
endeavor. This will be elaborated on in Section
II. The thrust of the argument, to recapitulate,
is that in social work, social goals, growth goals,
and individual goals are interrelated and that
social systems and their component human systems
are interacting through feedback loops, therefore,
to postulate that groupwork is applicable to one
narrowly defined kind of group is untenable.

It is contended here that purpose and contract
guide the process and method, not labels such as
goal-oriented, or growth-oriented treatment, Purpose and contract are always related to goals. The
specifics of method and variables involved will
vary according to purpose, size, composition, and
so on, but groupwork is groupwork as long as the
group process and group experience are the focii
of the group and the worker. The contract is an
agreement about purpose, means, and reciprocal role
expectations.

The Group Concept

It will be useful to examine another point of
view which is inherent in social work through group
process. In any social situation, such as in a
group or a family, it is inaccurate to think that
any one member influences another one directly.
Each member at all times within the social context
is being influenced by all of the other members as
well as by the collective. Every statement and
nonverbal action influences the process and, hence,
the balance of forces in the group. The group processes and the group forces are the media of influence. All action takes place within the context
of all of the influences and, therefore, there is
an emergent result which differs from either one

individual's influence or even the sum of individuals' influences. In a sense it is a compromise of alternatives but it is also something new and different from the totality of the components.

With this as a premise, and it is a valid one, the worker does not have a direct influence on any member, nor can he assume that he can be working on any one-to-one within the group setting. What he is doing or saying is only one among a myriad of influences on anyone at any given time, and his contribution is being acted upon and altered by the impact of multiple influences which intervene between him as the sender of a message and all of the receivers.

The worker who focuses on an individual in the group is not utilizing group process and, hence, is neglecting the very essence of the growth or therapeutic quality inherent in the group. But even more important, he ignores the influence that the group is having upon the effect of his acts. Such workers offer direct, individual interpretation; seek to develop an awareness of the possible links between the past and present behaviors of individuals; explore unconscious material; and evoke information through the group sessions upon which to base individual interpretations. However, a social worker who enables the group process encourages the group forces to operate and thereby makes it possible for any member in a group setting to experience his problems in an atmosphere in which he need not flee or maintain a wall around himself. The worker encourages mutual support and works to free the group so that it can provide corrective experiences, explore reality, test consequences of action, and find appropriate solutions.

Social work through group process relies upon group forces as the primary medium for growth and change. The function of the worker is to permit the group to become a supportive medium and to allow group processes to nurture and succor each member. The focus of the work is upon the group and the group processes.

This conception is applicable and amenable to social work with groups. As such, it is very different from casework in a group, or group casework.

It is the group, the forces within the group, and the group process which are the primary media in the use of groups in social work.

Resumé

Section I has set forth a variety of group designs currently used in social work with some explanation of the theory or fragments of theory that seem to underlie each. Where possible, the assumptions or hypotheses have been educed. Some aspects of these designs have been rejected and the reasons given. In other instances they have been accepted as appropriate to social work and its values, and in keeping with modern theory of the behavior of individuals and social organizations.

A small beginning has been made in the establishment of a model for groupwork, especially the ideas that individuals, groups, and communities are inextricably interrelated; that psychological, social, and cultural subsystems are both psychological and social; that in social work, groupwork is the way the worker enables social and group process to achieve social work objectives, and it is the group process and group experience that are central in the practice; that treatment groups, or social-change groups are goal-oriented groups, and that a major determinant of function, structure, and method is purpose.

As this section comes to an end, it is an important bridge to Section II to reaffirm that social work is focused on both the person and the environment; it functions in relating the person to his environment in ways which are constructive to both. One way of describing this focus is to speak of the transaction between the individual and the environment. The transaction is the means through which an individual has his needs met and people maintain an environment conducive to other persons having their needs met.

The task now is to endeavor to construct a groupwork model.

CHAPTER 3

FOUNDATION STONES FOR A WORKING MODEL
FOR GROUP METHODS IN SOCIAL WORK

As we have said before, the theoretical under-pinnings for almost all of the groupwork designs extant place major emphasis on one or another set of variables. While lip service is given to the relationship among the various subsystems, that is, psychological and environmental, the present leading designs rest upon monolithic frames of reference. Many writers recognize the existence of systems other than the one to which they give primacy but rarely, if ever, do they demonstrate the interdependence of other subsystem variables.

While it is true that persons are in situations, which gives rise to the phrase "person-in-situation" in the literature, the situation is also in the person. We are in large part the sum total of our experiences and have incorporated into ourselves the environment, relationships, and role models; we have been "programmed" by the input from the impinging world. Social caseworkers tend to view the person against a backdrop and, while they admit the influence of social factors, the individual is seen separately from them. Community organization writers tend to fail to see the people. More recently, social workers who are relying upon organizational theory seem to have chosen to eliminate the internal mechanisms of the human actor. However, Katz and Kahn note, "The uniformity, the routinization, and the fragmentation of behavior run counter not only to the factor of individual differences but to the needs of people for self-determination, spontaneity, and accomplishment, and the expression of individual skills and talents."[1]

There is really no excuse or justification today for any theorist in the field of human behavior to disregard the individual as a psycho-

---

[1]Daniel Katz and Robert L. Kahn, The Psychology of Organizations, (New York: John Wiley & Sons, Inc., 1966), p. 80.

logical system. Psychiatry, psychology, and, of course, social work are moving more and more toward understanding and using group, organization, and community factors in comprehending and enhancing individual behavior. Yet at a time when serious students of behavior are demonstrating the inseparability of psychological and social components in human behavior, some social scientists and social workers are building models predicated solely on variables external to the individual. This seems strange when at the same time systems theory has become recognized as a viable construct for analyzing social behavior.

This book does not rely wholly on social systems theory nor is the model presented in it offered as a systems model. It incorporates some of the tenets of a systems approach and the theory may be said to run through this model as an integrating theme.

At this writing, one hears that some faculty members in accredited schools of social work are suggesting the removal of individual psychology from the human growth and social environment courses in the curriculum. Such a suggestion seems to me to be preposterous in the light of (1) the hard data we have about behavior; (2) the social thought of our time, that is, involvement, participating democracy, and egalitarianism; (3) research studies which have found that different therapies work equally well or are equally ineffective but that relationship seems to be an essential therapeutic ingredient; (4) social systems theory. The behavioral theorists might argue here that reinforcement and operant conditioning do not need motivation as a concept or relationship, but while they can demonstrate behavioral change, we have yet to assess the costs of such change. I am not rejecting behavioral theory, but I am insisting that it be related to the psychological economy of the individual. I believe that the constructs of predisposition, precipitation, and perpetuation must be taken into consideration.[1] The predisposing factors are genetic, psychological, and social; that is to say that they are biological and hereditary. They are developed also through the interrelation

---

[1]Alexander H. Leighton, <u>My Name Is Legion.</u>

and matching of resources to needs throughout life stages as well as through learning.

A point to be stressed is that groups form and act because they can find group goals and actions which are ego-syntonic through collective activity even though the individual members have needs and motives which are different from each other's.

It is important for groupworkers to realize that the range of normal behavior has been conceptualized from two basic positions in order to present a modal personality in a given culture. On the one hand the members of a group have their individual motives which are linked to needs and goals. Large numbers of people within a given culture can be characterized by statistically average needs, motives, and hence, behavioral responses. An example in our context might be the needs and motives of adolescent boys, black, from a low income, ghetto area in a northern, urban center. A social worker might assume that these needs, motives, and responses could be summed up in a normative personality and hypothesize that the boys could be jointly and severally served in a certain type of group, with certain kinds of programs, and within certain kinds of relationships.

On the other hand, one can fashion a social model which explains behaviors by inferring values and social norms which sanction specific behavioral responses and then ascribe needs and motives to them. Neither approach can provide adequate guides for the utilization of program or methods, nor will the combination of the two prove more useful.

One of the dangers and serious limitations of these kinds of formulations such as "modal" personalities, is a groupwork practice predicated on normative needs so that individual assessments are disdained. Also, most of the organizational and social models have to do with probability considerations and such considerations never explain individual cases nor guide one in helping an individual and his environment to match.

Behavior is only symptomatic. By observing behavior and applying theoretical knowledge we

can get some understanding of what the behavior
means. We must always ask ourselves what the person is expressing: what is the message contained
in his aggressiveness or shyness, in his choice of
program activity, in his role performance? The
social worker who works with groups must peer beyond and below the statistical averages or modalities, the social structure, and the program, and
seek to learn the meanings they hold for the members. Unless he understands them as individuals
within a social situation, he cannot assist them
to satisfy their needs, enjoy their lives, learn,
or use themselves in socially constructive ways.

It is about time that all the little blind
men who have been examining tactually the prover-
bial elephant and have limited this to a very
small segment of the epidermis, meet in a group,
share their findings, and put them together so as
to come up with a conception of reality that has
a semblance of reality.

Because the model that is to be constructed
here rests so heavily on the idea of the interrelationship of psychological and social variables, it is necessary to develop the premise more
fully than has already been done, even though
some of it may seem to be repetitious.

I am not suggesting that no one has put forward the interrelationship of psychic variables
and social variables. Psychology: A Study of a
Science, Volume III, deals with "Formulations of
the Person and the Social Context."[1] In this work
Rappaport, Rogers, Parsons, and others delineate
what they consider to be independent variables,
dependent variables, and intervening variables.
The material, while imposing and important, does
not quite come off because the writers do not explain how these variables interact with each
other. The book is important, however, because it
does make many of the variables explicit and it
does not limit itself to classical psychoanalytic
theory.

I acknowledge these efforts to develop a

----

[1]Sigmund Koch, Psychology: A Study of a
Science, Vol. III (New York: McGraw-Hill Book
Co., 1959).

model for human behavior. What I am arguing is that social work has not applied the interrelated approach in its middle-theory or operational-theory models, and it does not utilize it in its treatment practice to the extent that it could or it should. I also insist that most of the groupwork designs that have been presented in Section I rest upon single subsystem dynamics and that the authors may give lip service to a broader approach but they do not, in fact, spell one out. The group is an obvious enactment of individual and social-system interaction and, therefore, groupwork cannot be anything else but a method and process that uses several sets of variables to explain what is going on, and also to facilitate the most efficacious matching of them so that the potentials of the members may be maximized.

Systems theorists have helped us to see that the dynamics of physical systems differ from those of social systems. For instance, our biological organism is predicated upon physical and chemical processes while a social system involves psychological and communication processes. Individuals are psychological but it is my contention that the social and psychological systems are interpenetrating and that individuals are social and social entities are psychological. The group is a psychological and social organization. The individual is a social-physical-psychological system which grows and functions through interactions with other similar person-systems. The person and his social context meld into an emergent system. Unless this is understood, it is easy to fall into the error of analyzing social systems with constructs from mechanical models.

The interrelation of the psychological and social processes which operate through communication creates an entity which we call a group.

The group as a social system operates by virtue of the fact that its components are people and as such they have options, make choices, and experience variety. It is the free choice to operate on differential options that determines group movement and directions, group decisions, and group processes. Whether the member is free to make choices and is self-determining, or whether he is viewed as predetermined and programmed by virtue of what he is and the rigidities of the structure of the social system, is a fruitless argument. He is both, for

this is a question of complementary opposites.
Both are true and both are false. He has free
choices within predetermined limits and it is a
thesis of this book that our goal is to elaborate
and expand the options and free the capacity to
make choices.

Norms and role expectations can prescribe
only ranges of accepted behaviors. Behavior can
be altered within ranges so as to be less self-
defeating and less injurious to others, hence,
more gratifying and socially constructive.

For purposes of this discussion, a group is
a system which can be visualized on a three-
dimensional chart as made up of the needs, predispositions, learnings, motives, goals, and so
on of each individual member intersecting, overlapping, meeting, and opposing the paths of other
members; and the behaviors are the attempts of
each to meet his needs and reach personal goals
while going through the maze. The pathways are
not laid out like air corridors and, hence, movement can be in any direction. The choice of direction, speed, and force, therefore, must depend
upon the individual pilot, the condition of his
vehicle, the forces in the field, the alternatives available, and the goals sought.

In order to relate this orientation to social
work, we refer to Bartlett. She says, "In seeking to understand the situation, the social worker
is concerned with both the inner and outer aspects,
the personality, and the social environment. This
is a broader and more balanced view of the person-
in-situation than is sought by most disciplines,
which usually confine themselves to one perspective on behavior....

"While the social worker must analyze complex
situations and deal with parts in seeking to bring
about change, there is a strong tendency to bring
the parts together to perceive the person and the
situation as a whole."[1]

---

[1]Harriett M. Bartlett, "Characteristics of
Social Work," Building Social Work Knowledge:
Report of a Conference (New York: National Associ-
ation of Social Workers, 1964).

While no one would contradict this statement, the fact is that social workers use many such means in trying to understand a situation but not nearly as many in treating it. In treatment, it tends to be an either/or, a tandem, or a sequence, rather than a unified strategy. Of this Gordon writes, "While social work has historically maintained a focus on both individual and environment, there have been significant imbalances, first primarily toward environment, later toward individual behavior under the impact of psychoanalytic theory, and more recently toward the social, cultural, and economic environment under the impact of ideas from these disciplines."[1] One might also add the political sciences.

The major concepts for relating the two systems have not been identified and there has been little research in social work or even investigation of the question. Role has been offered as the main integrative concept to bridge the two, but social work hardly uses role theory in treatment. Gordon suggests, "The quantity and quality of this transaction between individual and environment is seen as a critical factor in an individual having his needs met and in the maintenance of an impinging environment conducive to other individuals having their needs met. The quantity and quality of transaction is itself dependent on a substantial degree of matching of an individual's coping patterns and the quality of the impinging environment; the more nearly matched, the greater the quantity and the better the quality of the transaction for meeting the needs of individuals. With these constructs then, a preliminary definition of social work would be that it is the profession concerned with the matching of coping patterns and qualities of the impinging environment which permit the amount and kind of transaction required for individuals to satisfy their needs and to contribute to an environment in which others may also meet their needs."[2]

This formulation rests upon a value, namely,

---

[1] Gordon, "Constructs for Organizing Social Work Knowledge."

[2] Ibid.

that social goals or social change are for the good of individuals. We are not creating better groups, organizations, communities, or societies as ends in themselves, but as enhancing environments for human beings. Gordon goes on, "The definition of social work would then be that it is a profession concerned with the matching of coping patterns and qualities of impinging environment to provide the quality and quantity of transaction required for individuals to realize the maximum of their human potential and maintain an environment conducive to the maximum realization of all individuals."

Is what has been said thus far pure philosophy? "The Stirling County Study of Psychiatric Disorder and Socio-Cultural Environment," which was a vigorous empirical study, concludes that the most clearly and directly noxious aspects of socio-cultural disintegration are those that affect the achievement of love, recognition, spontaneity, and a sense of belonging to a moral order and of being right in what one does.[1] I think it is safe to extrapolate and say that these things are apparently needs for human beings.

While it is true that there is no unified theory of behavior and we lack the major concepts for relating the various subsystems, we do have some useful approaches.[2] I suspect that we like to say that we have no unifying concepts because we prefer to stay in our own corners. It is much easier to predicate operations on single-concept systems than to try to handle a large construct. Social scientists are looking for a very complicated, erudite, and all-embracing theory. After all, human beings and their societies are complex. It is because social scientists are seeking something that is a perfect theory that they can deprecate operational theory and scoff at experience and wisdom knowledge. Social workers ought not

---

[1]Alexander Leighton et al, The Character of Danger (New York: Basic Books, Inc., 1963), p. 388.

[2]Such as Alfred Kuhn's, A Study of Society: A Unified Approach (Homewood, Ill.: Irwin-Dorsey Press, 1963).

to be influenced by such seeking for Nirvana, nor
can they afford to be. Social workers need to
work to enhance functioning and to effect change
while social science examines what happens. There
is ample evidence to support more simplistic but
working models and it is these operational theories that social work must develop and use. All
theory must be rigorously tested empirically, to
be sure. There is much need to observe and describe and greater need to explain, but if theories work, even though simplistic, let us not be
so ready to knock them.

Needs and Responses; Resources and Responses

There are, in the above context, human needs
which are considered to be universal. The significance of such needs varies from life stage to
life stage.[1] Any need varies in intensity and in
its influence on behavior, depending upon the age
and predisposition of the person. People, of
course, are different. If needs vary in time
stages, resources to meet such needs must also be
varied so that needs and resources "cog-wheel,"
or match.

Needs are assessed differently by different
people; for example, Adler postulates behavior on
a need to feel important, Sullivan on interpersonal
relations, Fairbain on object relations, White on
relationship with the environment. Towle provided
a continuum of needs based upon self-realization.[2]
These range from (1) basic, physical, survival
needs through (2) security, (3) belongingness, (4)
love and esteem to (5) self-realization needs.
Needs occur in importance, according to Maslow, in
that sequence of priority. He argues that an individual is not concerned with esteem, nor can he
be appealed to in these terms until he has minimum
and continuing satisfaction with his survival, security, belongingness, and love needs. At any
given time all five needs are present, but one
need is dominant or most powerful. The individ-

---

[1]Leighton, My Name Is Legion.

[2]A. H. Maslow, Motivation and Personality
(New York: Harper & Brothers, 1954).

ual's first unsatisfied need in the order of relative priority becomes his dominant need. Any critical change in the individual, in the external situation in which he finds himself, or in both, may cause a shift of that individual's dominant need along that continuum. Parenthetically, if the groupworker or group is offering need-meeting resources which do not fit the dominant need, it is not really a resource. This has important connotations in social work practice.

The individual, Maslow believes, directs his behavior toward satisfying the need that is dominant at any given time. Motivation is based upon needs, actions, the goals toward which behavior is directed, and the energy released in the individual to accomplish these goals. The energy of the individual increases with the intensity of his need. These five needs merge into each other and there is no clear line of demarcation between them. The individual's dominant need may change from situation to situation. The individual's behavior, generally, gains at least partial satisfaction of more than one need at a time. The fact that many basic needs are present and that all of these needs influence the behavior of an individual helps one to explain needs and responses.

Parenthetically again, if one manipulates social-system variables which are external to the individual, one can threaten or calm such things as survival-, security-, love-, and belongingness-need responses and by so doing, perhaps unwittingly, bring into dominance different needs. Also, people in a group are at different levels in their need dominance and, hence, the manipulation of external variables will impact differently on each member. This may seem obvious, but it is disregarded by many theorists. By like token, in Maslow's terms, learning and conditioning must be related as functions of motivation.

Thomas and Goodman prefer to disregard motivation but they observe that the type of reinforcement presented is an important variable. The reinforcer must be determined empirically by observing changes in the strength of the response to it. We know, of course, that certain reinforcers derive their potency from having been paired previously with primary reinforcers. Thomas and

Goodman suggest that for a program to change behaviors the worker carefully select those reinforcers to which the client will respond.[1] I think such reinforcers are need meeters, or can be classified as secondary gains and I am inclined to believe that, as such, they are motivators. Perhaps these writers believe that reinforcers are learned, but learned or not, they do motivate. The secondary reinforcers may develop through pairing with primary reinforcers but, as such, they are symbolic need meeters even if they are learned through conditioning.

It may be that needs are arranged on a continuum and that their position in a hierarchy is fixed, as Maslow suggests. I prefer to think of them as related to each other in a different way. The needs most often identified in social work are: to be loved, to be recognized, to have status, to be secure, to belong, to be accepted, and to feel adequate. These are not listed in any order. To some individuals, to belong means that one is accepted, important, and liked by others. Depending on to what one belongs, status may accrue. To have status makes one feel adequate and recognized; it connotes acceptance. To be loved affords security.

I am not placing them in any fixed set of relationships but suggesting that they vary in their importance to individuals and that in given situations the effort to satisfy one need may imply the striving to satisfy other needs. Needs vary greatly from person to person, and for each person from social situation to social situation. We can, however, relate this back to Leighton's findings that love, recognition, and a sense of belonging are important needs which are susceptible to provision or deprivation in the social environment with notable effects on mental well-being.

However one wishes to classify them, the points being made here are as follows:

1. Behavior results from the organism's efforts to meet certain needs.

---

[1]Thomas and Goodman, <u>Socio-Behavioral Theory and Interpersonal Helping in Social Work.</u>

2. The needs of individuals differ in primacy, intensity, predispositions, time, and satisfyers.

3. Different kinds of behavior mean different things in different people.

4. A given behavior can be caused by different needs in the same person and in different people; a given need may result in a wide variety of behaviors in the same person and in different people.

5. If the individual needs to feel loved and the worker gives recognition--for example, by hanging a picture the person has painted--which is not perceived by the individual as love or is not loving, the giving of recognition in that situation is not need-meeting because the response or resource does not match the need and is not a specific at the time.

Explicitly, a need affects behavior which seeks to satisfy that need, that is, the individual responds to his need by behaving and as such it is a need-meeting response. The impinging environment responds by satisfying, ignoring, frustrating, or endangering the person; that is a second response. Such a response from the environment acts upon the organism and produces more behavior which may be quiet due to satisfaction, or violent due to frustration, or withdrawn due to fear or anxiety, and so on. Bion characterized these behavioral responses as fight, flight, dependency, and pairing.[1] He suggested that as a result of the perpetuating factors of the environment, a pattern of response could become a mode or habit for behavior in a group; that is to say, that the group as an impinging environment could elicit certain modal behavior from its individual members by the kind of responses it made to the individual's need-satisfying attempts or by virtue of the kind of an environment the individual perceived it to be.

The available resources, also, influence the

---

[1] W. R. Bion, Experiences in Groups and Other Papers (New York: Basic Books, Inc., 1961).

behavior of the individual. Resources can meet
needs or frustrate them and, hence, a second set
of behaviors are affected by the resources. Needs
produce behavior, responses to the need-seeking-
gratification behavior produce behavior, and resources produce behavior with the group (and in
general). It seems then that there is a very important relationship between needs and the impinging environment. The environment can produce,
change, and perpetuate behavior; it can affect different people differently, depending upon their
need structures, their satisfaction-seeking response to their needs, the reaction or response of
the environment, and the resources available. It
seems that we could alter the whole system by influencing any one of the components in that interrelated set and, in turn, influence all the other
components.

The need dispositions of each individual are
predicated upon genetics and past experiences
which predispose and develop habits or modes of
adaptation and defenses. Past experiences and
genetics influence self-concept and set up the
primacy of certain needs and satisfactions. They
influence wishes, preferences, desires, fears,
anxieties, and are important also in the formulation of goals.

The situation (which can be the group experience) can precipitate that which is predisposed
by acting upon the predetermined-action-mechanisms
of the individual. All experiences during a lifetime become part of the person or part of his ego
and are the imperatives that define the range of
options and choices that are available to him as
his responses. The situation (which can be the
group experience) can perpetuate the behavioral
modes by reinforcing them or can effect change by
virtue of adding to the bank of experiences, providing new options, providing varied choices, and
rewarding new behaviors. It can also eliminate
behaviors by filtering out old enforcers or blockers.
The cog-wheeling of group structure with individual structure can enhance by matching or it can
endanger through faulty meshing and deprivation.

The structure of a group (the social variables) are not the factors that determine the behavior of the members as simple cause and effect.

They are important variables only in relation to their meaning to the individual, and their meaning is a question of need dispositions, need-meeting potentials, and consequences.

We are going to examine some of the elements in group structure such as position, status, role, norms, and demonstrate how, although they are group properties which are external to the psychological individual, they interact with the need dispositions of the persons in a group.

POSITION IS A STRUCTURAL VARIABLE. Position in some groups provides access to resources as well as control of resources. To some it can mean recognition of adequacy and hence worth. For some, it can buy being liked or at least the appearance of being liked. Low position can be depriving, depreciating, and isolating. Position allows one to be validated, and perhaps to be self-realizing. Position, then, is a means to need-meeting and also can allow or deny the right to behave as one needs to or wants to. By access and control of resources, an individual can have many more options, but high position can also be frightening, anxiety-producing, and need-defeating. The high gastric-acid producer in a high position increases his chances of suffering from an ulcer.

Position, to be enhancing, must match the need dispositions of the occupant of the position. If one has a position and cannot produce that which the organization demands, the individual can be damaged easily. Some positions are high risk and fit competitive, skilled, hyperactive persons but are devastating to others.

Position locates people in the communication network. The higher and more central the position, the more information is directed to one. This fact alone makes one feel part of the group. In reverse, those not in the communication channels feel left out and are peripheral. They feel they do not belong, are not important, and are lacking in power.

If the person who is peripheral has a low self-image and his position confirms or enforces that image, he may revel in his unhappiness if that is his nature, or he may enjoy being an isolate,

68

especially if he is afraid of relationships.

If a person never belonged in his family and has had little sense of belonging all through his life, he may settle into a peripheral position and be content to seem to belong. How much one needs to belong, to have status, and to be recognized may determine how one responds to one's position, or how one strives for position, or how one frustrates others' occupancy of positions. If a person does not need to be reaffirmed by position--does not have any primacy of need for status, power, importance, and sense of belonging because he is secure in knowing he has or can have all of these things at will--high office may mean nothing and he may be happy and useful and even motivated in an unimportant position. The meaning of position also varies considerably from culture to culture and group to group. It is certainly true that reinforcers vary from individual to individual, setting to setting, and culture to culture.

All men are not economic men. Some seek expression through art, service, love of fellowman, freedom, or being loved. Organizational structure is effective only insofar as it rewards the universal needs and desires, but when it fails to match the need dispositions of its individual members, it wastes the motive potentials.

The important considerations here are position, need disposition, as well as responses and cultural values in interaction. In and of itself, position is meaningless.

STATUS IS A STRUCTURAL VARIABLE. Status is closely related to position although they are often confused. Status is the rank or importance that other people give to one and it also connotes the rank or importance that one believes others afford to him or that one thinks one has. It is a relative term because one has status in relation to someone else, that is, higher or lower than others or another. Status can apply to a position, a person, or a function. However, status and position are not linked solidly together. The father, which is a position, may have high status in one family and low status in another; high in one culture, low in another; the position of the father may be high in a family but the father's illness may reduce him to a low status.

A person's position, previous experience, or cultural bias may lead him to think that he has high status (or deserves it) and yet he may be regarded lowly by others. Obviously, one's self-image, bearing, aggressiveness, verbalization, energy output, and production will be influenced by one's status. One's performance depends on the kind of status one believes one has. If one thinks one has high status but others do not respond, one will be frustrated, angered, in conflict, and might behave in a fight, flight, or dependency fashion.

However, how one responds to the kind of status one has is directly related to the meaning status has for one. If one's need for status is primary, high status in the group can meet the need and produce adequate competence. If one needs to feel important, needs to be bolstered, needs to be validated, one's behavior in the group will vary with the status one has; that is, one will strive to improve one's status, or will react negatively if it is low, or will be comfortable and productive if it is high. If one has great need for security, high status may produce feelings of high risk and be threatening. Different people respond to status and status-seeking differently. Status has no real meaning as a variable independent of the meaning that it has to the individual and to the other individuals in the group who are responding.

We are saying that all people do not need status in the same way, that status means different things to different people; that is, it can mean recognition to one, adequacy to another, a chance for realization to still another, that at different stages and times it has a different meaning to the same person, and that in any case the responses to it differ. Status has meaning only insofar as it meets the need disposition and goal orientation of a person, and is the proper resource for him. To apply Gordon's formulation, a certain status in the structure is to be desired for a given individual when it helps the individual maximize his potential and in so doing he, in turn, maximizes the capacity of the group to maximize the potentials of all of the other members.

It is possible to view the structure in a

70

different way; that is, if the group is to be effective in achieving its group goal (task) it
needs certain positions, and also certain status
allocations. It has been demonstrated that if
members of a board of directors of a certain social agency feel that their positions do not ap-
proximate their own assessment of their statuses,
they do not contribute and finally drop out. If
a person is placed in a position or given status
he does not want or that fails to meet his needs,
he does not contribute as much as he could and he
can become a blocker or a dropout. This prevents
the group from achieving its goal.

L. K. Frank suggests, and I agree, that people join groups to meet their needs.[1] Rensis
Likert holds that motivation in organizations is
directly related to ego recognition and the realization of each individual in the organizational
structure.[2] Skinner's pigeons would not have performed so admirably, I suspect, had their needs
not been met.

ROLE IS A STRUCTURAL VARIABLE. Much has been
written about the role concept and it is alleged
that role is the bridge or integrating link between psychological and social systems. Helen
Perlman has built a book around the role concept
in social work.[3] Social workers use the concept
to describe social functioning, and sometimes base
a psycho-social diagnosis on such ideas as role
conflict, role reversal, role gap, and the like.
Groupworkers talk about group roles meaning much
the same as the group dynamics people do; that is,
such roles as opinion seeker, opinion giver, information giver, gatekeeper, and so on. Certain
authors suggest that a wide role repetoire is
characteristic of mature social functioning. Some

---

[1]L. K. Frank, "What Influences People to Join
Organizations," _Adult Leadership_ (January, 1958).

[2]Rensis Likert, _Motivation: The Core of
Management_ (New York: American Management Association, 1953).

[3]Helen Perlman, _Persona, Social Role and
Personality_ (Chicago: University of Chicago Press,
1968).

suggest that the learning of roles and role expectations is an important aspect of groupwork. Little has been demonstrated about role theory and treatment to support the allegation that role is an integrating theme in practice. The concept of role has many facets and, unfortunately, as is often the case, sociologists write about role differently than do social psychologists. Role is the actual behavior of an actor but it is also the expectation that others hold for the actor. Role is directly related to the position one occupies, and the status one holds. In a given culture, for example, the father is a position. The position of the father calls for certain behaviors and, hence, a father's role behavior is prescribed and expected. How the father, in fact, behaves is also the father's role. In some cultures, the status of a person--not necessarily the status of his position--also prescribes certain behavior. Status and position are not synonymous terms or ideas. A position is locus in a structure while status is the importance the position and/or the person has.

The role expectation held for a position and/or a status may or may not be compatible with the needs and capabilities of the occupant of that position and if the role does not provide the actor with satisfaction, frustration may result. If the role expectations exceed the capabilities of the actor, anxiety may follow as well as the probability of the failure to achieve. Such a failure influences one's sense of adequacy and also one's self-image. Rogers and Dymond have given some convincing arguments which relate mental health to self-image, and one could extrapolate in the same sense the possibilities inherent in a role for a given individual as the role enhances or depreciates his image.[1]

Then, if the role expectation for a position or status does not meet the needs of the occupant, or frustrates him by too little or too great a demand, he will experience grave discomfort. His role enactment may meet the expectations and be satisfying in most ways, but afford the individual

---

[1]E. R. Rogers and R. F. Dymond, **Psychotherapy and Personality Change** (Chicago: University of Chicago Press, 1954).

no status or no recognition. On the other hand, it may suit his personality but not his economic needs. The social environment and his needs do not match in such instances.

Through past experience or value orientations, the individual may misread the expectations, or he may have an ideal expectation for himself in the position or status which he is unable to fulfill. Measured against his own standard he falls short of his own expectations, self-image suffers, frustration ensues, and a sense of achievement is lacking.

It is possible that a social structure denies access to certain role enactments because of the individual's lack of power, lack of status, class, or caste. The roles that might most meet his needs or provide maximum satisfaction are not made available. That person's potential cannot be maximized because of social restraints or limitations. It might be that the role needed does not exist in that group or social structure and again the person is denied a need-meeting and growth experience. Such social deficiencies and limits can by habituation warp the individual's personality, restrict his development of role repetoires, set behavioral patterns that repeat themselves and, thereby, freeze the person into inappropriate or thwarting life situations. People tend to react or re-enact habitual group roles so that each new group setting finds them redoing what they have done in recent, previous groups. Such behavior seems to be reinforced even though it has failed to be satisfying in the past. It seems to be reinforced because it gives security, or often because it permits one to belong, or to think it is the ticket for belonging.

Quite often the group casts people into roles because the powerful and high-status members need to have others perform certain roles, or sometimes because these roles express the group's psychological conflicts, climate, or culture. Kai Erikson, the son of Erik Erikson, has demonstrated for example, that groups may cast persons into a deviant role. We know that group emotion will sometimes unconsciously direct a member to challenge authority, act out, be smutty to meet the group urge, or act to release group tension.

Such group phenomena may meet the actor's desires by triggering the behavior, but at the same time it may cause a breakthrough of repressed urges and, hence, unsocialize the person and cause him to be punished or to punish himself through his guilt feelings.

The role enactments and the group's influences on role enactments, therefore, can be matching or discordant. A person's need dispositions may be served or thwarted, and in serving may be growth-producing or socially punishable. We are discussing role then as the transaction between the individual, his psychological needs and habits, the demands of the group (social situation), and the opportunities it affords.

It is true also that in addition to groups assigning roles to members as we have been discussing, members choose roles through habit or in response to needs. Such choices are usually not conscious or cognitive, but are made because the person is seeking to meet his needs; or because his preferences are influenced by his personality based upon past experiences, social learning, and modes of adaptation. Such choices are not necessarily rational and may be maladaptive, self-defeating, or based upon distorted perceptions.

As we said before, a person may not know what is expected of him. He can be shown or taught. He may know what is expected but lack the skill needed to perform. The skill can be taught or trained. He may know what is expected and have the skill but not want to perform. Attitudes, values, and desires can be changed through identification, group experience, re-education, goal changes, and so forth. He may know, have skill, and want to perform but be blocked or psychologically unable to do so. Each of these situations requires a different approach but all, in one way or another, depend upon the individual and how he thinks, feels, and functions.

Role-teaching, or casting people into roles without regard for the compatibility of the role expectations and for a person's physical and psychological predispositions can precipitate unhappy results. A corollary follows that social work through group process must utilize group roles in the service of the members.

Suppose, if you will, that a high gastric-acid secreter who is ulcer prone is elevated to a position fraught with tension, conflict, and insecurity. Suppose that a woman who is dependent and lacks self-confidence is abandoned by her spouse and becomes the head of her household of several small children, must become the bread-winner, and then is selected to be a delegate to a citizen's neighborhood council. Suppose that a Cuban-refugee physician is denied a medical license in this country and he becomes an orderly in a hospital. All of these situations have counter-parts in group life, organizational life, in the ward, on the board, in the staff, and in the social work practice group. We are trying to illustrate that such easy solutions as teaching a role, or changing positions and status, hence, role expectations, can throw some people into states of anxiety, physical difficulty, withdrawal, or acting out.

In contrast, psychological insights and restructuring may enable role performances which the social situation will not condone, will punish, will frustrate, or will undo.

Socialization and the life styles which a culture adopts are conducive to educating or training for roles which the culture prefers or requires. In this way the social group life molds the personality. It can be said that lower-income fathers displace their frustration and hostility on their sons. These men work at unsatisfying jobs wherein they are subject to repressive and capricious authority. In order to survive in their environmental and occupational settings, they must be either submissive and accept the authority of harsh foremen, or they must be hard and very aggressive to get and hold jobs.

Certainly, the men do not reason out and consciously plan to create sons who can follow in their footsteps but, actually, this is what happens. By displacing their own disappointments on their sons, the sons become accustomed to dictatorial bosses and either submit or fight. In some grand design, a society tends to create the kinds of people it needs to make it run. Our industrial and stratified society needs cog-type workers; fathers train their sons to fit into this complex and enact roles that are available to them.

The fact is that these roles do not meet the needs of the fathers. They perpetuate destructive life styles and exploit people for the so-called good of the group. These men are unhappy and unfulfilled, but they are cast into self-perpetuating roles. This is what we have done to our black people, our American Indians, and our Mexican itinerant workers, for example.

Some people think that all we have to do is manipulate the variables of position, status, role, and power and poor people will change their behaviors and become self-supporting, middle-class workers. Social work is characterized by a deep and all-abiding respect for people. The kinds of programs that are predicated upon single-purpose change such as advocated by job training, occupational opportunities, or role change, are not kind or in the best interests of the people because they fail to take into account the interrelationship of social and psychological variables. As roles are changed, people must be helped to fit these roles, and also must be fitted to roles they can perform with beneficial results to themselves as well as to their communities.

People do not transact with a society, or with a community. A culture is not transmitted or coped with through such large conceptual units. People transact with small groups in which they love, work, play, and acculturate. What has been said in this section about role applies basically to group roles and it is the small groups within which one plays out one's life that are the impinging environment. The group in social work is a medium, an environment, a milieu, a life space, a stage, and a laboratory. As such it is a slice of life and is the setting in which the learning, the matching, and the action takes place.

As with position and status, role is a psychosocial concept and in practice cannot be dealt with in any one dimension alone. Structural variables permit access to resources. They are environmental. In groupwork, they can be altered by

76

the group as a means of enhancing the functioning of the member. Such modifications are not only ends; that is, the end is not only the structural modification which may help the group function better, but they are the means whereby the individuals are helped.

Some persons fail to negotiate life's maze and are unable to interact appropriately with others or transact with the environment because they are unable to perceive, or assess their own position and that of others, their status and that of others, the role expectations and demands of themselves and others, and are naive about their own performance. Through feedback and group experience, they can learn some or all of these things and especially can they learn to "map" the group. They can learn to know, to assess feelings and attitudes as well as beliefs and values. They can be helped to gain self-awareness, to learn appropriateness, how rewards are gained, how status is earned, and how adaptive their own behavior is; that is, how appropriate their behavior is, how successfully they are coping, and wherein their behavior is malfunctional or self-defeating.

In these ways a person can be helped to alter behavior. In addition, such experience provides a means of validation for who one is, what one is, and how valuable or adequate one is. It provides identity confirmation and can be the means to identity change.

Change of any kind requires adaptation to change and also requires adaptability. It is axiomatic that if an organism does not or cannot adapt, it cannot survive. In its struggle for survival, its failure to adapt causes pain, frustration, and eventual disintegration. At the same time, life requires conflict and struggle with recurring crises that are negotiated and overcome in order to gain strength, skill, and increased capacity to cope with more challenging problems. Adaptation is not a static balance. It is a constantly spiralling process in which changes occur in the person and in the situation. The essence of social work through group process is adaptation to change. This is accomplished through feedback networks. The group feeds back to the members, and with help the members can self-adjust to the realities of interaction and transaction with the world. It is through this process that the individual is kept in touch with reality and through which reality-testing can be improved.

Group structure is the variable we have been discussing. Structure, as we have said, is relationships. Groups must develop a structure through which they function and the structure should be appropriate to the purpose of the group for most efficient operation. Task groups need a good deal of structure, usually because they function best when there is a clear-cut division of labor and responsibility, and communication networks channel information and feed back most efficiently to those who need it to perform the group roles. Structure informs the members about who is who and how to relate to each other, that is, how to behave in the interactions. Structure prescribes, dictates, and sets the rules for the interaction. Structure provides security; the security of knowing how to act.

People who need such security as a primary or dominant need require unambiguous and formal structure. For them, loose structure is anxiety-producing and frightening. It is not sufficiently accurate to state as a principle that the social worker when working with a group helps it to develop structure. It is more accurate to say that he enables it to develop a structure which is appropriate and that matches the needs of the members and the purpose of the group.

For persons who need freedom, self-realization, and human contact, rigid structure is limiting and irritating. Where people are afraid of each other, where they have difficulty in relating to people, they look for and demand structure. The greater the level of anxiety there is, the more demand for structure there will be. This is so because structure formalizes relationships. People can then confront one another as role players rather than as human beings. They can hide behind positions and statuses and avoid being themselves.

It is true that by allowing considerable structure, anxiety can be reduced. This may be flight and may be reinforcing social incompetence. If the purpose is to facilitate achieving a group task, such structuring may be desirable, but if the purpose is enhancing social functioning, per-

78

haps the members need to learn to deal with each other as people and not escape as role carriers.

The less structure a group provides, especially at its inception, the more the members will enact their usual modes of behavior, adaptation, defenses, and games because they will be reacting to stress, anxiety, fear, conflicts, and human contact. Bereft of structure they must be themselves, unprotected by a script. Such a living situation may afford maximum social learning.

Both learnings are essential; that is, people must learn a wide repetoire of roles and the appropriateness of behavior for positions, statuses, and given roles in order to be able to function in our society, but also, they must learn how to relate to others as people with intimacy and human warmth. Careful attention to structure and its use is essential in working with groups. One must be wary of universalized prescriptions and practice based upon group structure as the major medium for change.

Structure represents at best a convenient way of codifying and talking about certain apparent consistencies in social phenomena before their internal processes and dynamic laws are fully understood. Parsons cautioned that when we make structure the primary focus of our attention there is a danger that we will somehow reify it and bypass more basic questions about the processes that generate and maintain these apparent consistencies. Structure presupposes frozen process, but in reality process never freezes.

This book is committed to change, adaptation, and the freeing of people to be and to become. The unprincipled use of structure in working with groups can be a serious block to freedom. It can also defeat change. Once a group becomes structured, those in power resist change because they do not want to give up their access to resources and control over others. Persons with high status support each other and are not sensitive to the needs of those below them. They do not listen to them but send directives down to them. They cast others into roles needed by the high-status people with little regard for the role needs of the low-status people. Information is restricted to those in control. Such structuring develops subgroupings which then place barriers against the development of acceptances and affectional ties. Those who most need acceptance, a sense of self-worth and belonging, are deprived of these need-meeting resources. Group structure, when it is allowed to formalize as it usually does, can foster a most undemocratic process, become a subterfuge for control of others, a means of putting down, and a device for majority control to the detriment of the most incompetent, self-defeating, or powerless members of the group. If the people who need help are to get help in our groups, the question of group structure needs to be reviewed in groupwork. Moreover, positions that carry power, status that validates one's self, and roles that allow people to exploit others may be exactly the experiences in which many people should not be reinforced. Such experiences may be detrimental to them and to the common good. Also, it is obvious that such structuring does not help maximize the potentials for the others in the group.

All of these actual happenings in groups have been documented and validated by social research and group dynamics. This is how groups act. While I admit that my reaction is philosophical, I do not believe that people should be perpetuated in a need for structure to alleviate anxiety or as a channel to guide their interpersonal relations. Interpersonal relations, to be growth-promoting and need-meeting, require human encounter and closeness. When these are anxiety-producing, the lack is trust not structure. One can learn to trust structure to be sure, but that does not help one to learn to trust people.

It is my contention also that exploitation in any form is deleterious and that growth is not promoted in an atmosphere where people are denied access to the group's resources, no matter how high-sounding the words are that are used to justify it. Exploitation by the majority over the minority in the name of democratic process, pragmatism, or group goal, cannot be condoned in social work. It should not be condoned in any setting in our society.[1]

---

[1] Herbert J. Gans, "We Won't End the Urban Crisis until We End Majority Rule," New York Times Magazine, August 3, 1969.

NORMS, VALUES, AND STANDARDS ARE STRUCTURAL
VARIABLES. They also inform behavior. Norms are
one of the determinants in group composition because people tend to associate or choose others
whom they perceive share their own norms and values.
As soon as people come together and begin to form
a bond or group, group norms of behavior (and in
some instances attitudes) develop. The members
soon learn that one must conform to the norms which
are significantly central to the group's concerns
and purposes. Norms are enforced by contagion,
identification, incorporation, learning, sanctions,
and controls. If one wishes to continue to belong,
one conforms or at least behaves with conformation,
unless one can be accepted as a deviant or inno-
vator. Conformation here means acting on the
group's real values and desires and not on the
written or spoken ones necessarily. Even people
who are in leadership positions can be deposed if
they behave too far out of the group's norm range.

It is the very things being discussed here
which give a group so much power over a member and
make a group so influential in either changing behavior or keeping it constant. The more a person
needs to belong, the more power the group has over
him, and the more the group is a reference group,
the more the individual is likely to look to it
for his values. There are serious implications
for members of a group who want to get ahead. When
one needs to belong or needs to rise in the hierarchy, one tends to become part of the establishment and become sensitive to the power structure.
It has been said that the way to get along is to
go along. If one aspires to achieving status and
position in an organization, one is reluctant to
oppose or antagonize powerful members. There is
a breed of people who will risk such opposition
and who are loyal to their ideological commitments.
They act upon liberal convictions at the expense
of getting ahead. Imagine the emotional conflict
and the psychic cost to the man who is ideologically
liberal and yet needs to succeed or to feel accepted by the establishment.

However, here again the interrelationship of
the person and the social group is observed. If
one does not need to belong, a change in group norm
may result in his dropping out, whereas one who
needs to belong will conform. If the group is a

reference group; that is, if it is meeting important needs of a member, he will look to it for his values, otherwise he might not. The more central a person is in the affectional and communication network, the more he is likely to conform or internalize the value; the more peripheral he is, the less likely he will be to accept or act upon the values.

Norms and values that are held by at least three high-status people tend to dominate a group. However, people with strong convictions, great self-confidence and security, or who are challenging for position are not likely to conform. They will think for themselves.

It is easy to see the importance of group experience as an influence on norms, standards, values, and as a result on behavior. It should be apparent also from one's own experience that psychological sets, modes, and needs influence norms, standards, and values. Rigid people like tight norms. Cold people like values which deny the importance of human relationships. Sadistic people tend to applaud police brutality. Frustrated people hate minority groups. People who have problems with relationships subscribe to norms in a group that provide constitutions, by-laws, officers, and rules even where these have no possible validity for the particular group or its purpose. Parliamentary procedure was formulated for parliaments and not for groups of eight or ten people. Once again, the question of matching and group purpose is pertinent.

However, from a method point of view, alteration of norms and values changes behaviors, and maintenance of such patterns perpetuates behaviors. One questions whether value change is an end in itself or is a means of changing behavior in groupwork practice.

Values are based upon fundamental assumptions and beliefs and are related to individual goals. It has long been the premise of groupwork that it teaches values. Social workers contend that they believe in self-determination and hence value judgments do not enter into their practice. Of course, everyone knows that this is a euphemism, if not folklore. Social workers should not make value judgments but they do, and much practice denies self-determination more than it supports it. However, social groupwork has stated explicitly that it transmits values. This is inherent in socialization, of course.

The group has been characterized as a microcosm of the culture, that is, the members bring the outside culture into the group with them. The social agency is part of the educational or socializing institution of society. It is a form of social control, and as such it represents societal values, or at least the so-called dominant values. There is, of course, a great deal of "double standard" setting of norms in it, a great deal of hypocrisy and dishonesty, and much denial in the actual doing. The agency which sponsors the group and pays the worker represents the dominant values of society and has as a function the transmission of these values even in the most pristine of social agencies. To deny it is a hypocrisy in itself, and fails to take into account the intent of the board of directors, or the legislative body.

In social groupwork, the worker has been said to be a carrier of values, a symbol, and he therefore represents societal norms and values. Moreover, norms and values guide his role behavior, his interventions, his assessments, and diagnoses. Mental health, normality, and treatment modalities are based upon cultural assumptions which are value laden.[1]

I must raise the question now of whether it is helpful or even useful any longer to talk about the transmission of values in the way in which it has been promulgated in social groupwork for years. I do not wish to be definitive, or to answer the question, because this book is an argument against dogma of any kind. However, the question must be asked and an opinion or two given.

We are in an era characterized by great and rapid change, so fast in fact that social change which used to take twenty years or more now seems to happen in five years or even less. When social

---

[1]Jerome Frank, Persuasion and Healing (New York: Schocken Books, Inc., 1963), ch. 3.

change evolved more slowly, the lag in attitudes, values, and behaviors, although it existed, was not as pronounced or at least the culture was able to adjust to the realities more readily. The values that have been called dominant in urban America are obviously out-of-date. Perhaps they are not dead and they may return, but in many instances they certainly are inappropriate to current and future living. It is not the function of this book to go into this subject in any detail, but it must be looked at, even briefly, in order to decide what role social work has in value transmission.

1. The Protestant ethic grew out of the industrial revolution when it was deemed essential to get the masses to work long and hard. The urbanization that followed required a morality appropriate to the poor, huddled masses and the virtues of private property, thrift, chastity, marital fidelity and charity were extolled. In America, the Puritans found the right social climate to perpetuate the Protestant ethic as a new country had to be hewn out of the wilderness. People lived distances apart without a national police force and religion was the major institution for social control. The Protestant ethic is not appropriate in today's affluent society which is moving deeply into an automated and cybernetic age where work is about to become a drug on the market. The small family has replaced the large, the "pill" has altered morality, science has challenged religion, and an informed and educated population is asking the organized church some embarrassing questions.

2. Students have become aware that subject matter taught in the schools today as facts are not hard facts and much of what has been taught them is disproven even before they graduate. They are aware that the university is backing into the future with its eyes on the past, that college curricula will not do for the world as it is, as it ought to be, or as it will be. In our own field, social welfare systems are archaic and social treatment has fallen into disrepute because of its unwillingness to match the times. Schools of social work talk a great deal about change and innovation but are really performing the old play with a few new costumes and sets. Of all the institutions, they have been one of the slowest to change. Instead of education preparing students for adapta-

tion and adjustment to rapid change and flux, it clings to "facts," lecture halls, and the established social ways.

3. The church is only beginning to move from an emphasis on the hereafter to a concern for the here-and-now and the human condition. It has moved in this direction only because it has been forced to do so for survival and not because it lives by the values it preaches. As a result, in part, it has lost its role in social control and in value development. Most people reject the notion that "there will be pie in the sky when you die." Human relations and man's inhumanity are becoming recognized as more important than salvation.

4. Politics and government used to be called the "art of the possible." They have become the "science of options." Options, alternatives, action, and consequences are key, interrelated concepts that have importance in social work and will be discussed later. The ideals of democracy, namely, citizen participation and involvement, are becoming more accepted in practice than before. Here too, the human being is, coming to the fore.

5. Industry has found and is finding that things alone do not insure profits. Motivation through ego recognition, management through sensitivity training, and the switch from line and chain-of-command charts to group charts have been with us for some time. Now, however, industry is confronted with a revolution toward leisure, with automated production which will glut the market, and with the prospect of a vastly reduced consumer market if the workingman is no longer working or is working for only a few hours a day. All at once then, the idea of a guaranteed annual wage or a reverse income tax makes sense, and there is sudden interest in the retraining of people for service occupations.

6. Biological and physical progress has opened the way for transplants, artificial and changeable human parts, longer life, freezing people for future defrosting in a later century, test-tube babies, and thought control. These raise interesting and frightening ethical questions.

The purpose in listing a few of the many

changes taking place is to highlight the fact that the groupworker's values are probably out-of-date for the younger group members and that the norms and values of the typical social agency or sponsor are probably obsolete. The people who read this book in all probability will be professionally active in the year 2,000 and the children who are in today's groups will then be in the prime of their lives. The values the worker may be transmitting now are already old hat and certainly are not designed for the future. We just must realize that our own life experiences in growing up did not prepare us to set values for tomorrow. We have no idea what the world will be like.

However, having said that, we can help people to think through values, that is, to develop their own values that are relevant to reality. This process is accomplished by searching out and challenging basic assumptions and testing their appropriateness to reality, by seeking the alternatives and expanding the options, and by testing various consequences of differing actions. In such a confrontation, goals are important but goals must be matched by assumptions. It is part of the learning process to press for the assumptions that underlie the goals. Goals, values, and assumptions are related on feedback loops.

In addition, there are human values that inhere in our social work profession (often honored in the breach). These have to do with the value of the person, the dignity of people, freedom from domination by others, and the right to maximize one's potential. One of my students put it succinctly: "Instead of telling us that it is immoral to go to bed together, they might have told us that it is not right to exploit another person."

In social work, these values are not to be transmitted like a message over a telephone line. They are to be demonstrated in the relationships of worker and members. It may be that some workers will need to go back for retraining and it does mean that social work practice theory must readjust itself to a reaffirmation of human values. Control and manipulation have not only come into social work, but they have been accepted and rationalized in the literature. When the worker in a professional role interacts with a client in the client role, they do not encounter each other as two people but, instead, meet as two actors wearing theatrical masks. This will be discussed later at greater length. Members of a group can learn how to relate to each other in a meaningful encounter in a group if the group climate allows them to relate and if they are encouraged to do so by a worker. This is facilitated if both worker and members can be themselves and if the worker demonstrates by his behavior how people relate to each other as human beings.

COMMUNICATION IS A MAJOR PROCESS. People relate themselves to each other through communication; it is therefore a major process for interaction. Like role, communication is an integrating concept because it is both internal and external to the person. It is part of the social system and at the same time part of the psychology of each member.

Reduced to fundamentals, communication is a request, a request for personal need-meeting. It asks others to validate one, to attest that one exists, and to offer favorable response. One _is_ because others react to him. In this context, reality-based communication is essential for one to be in touch with, that is, in communication with reality. People learn to communicate in ways that secure survival. Communication is learned and it can be learned as real, as distorted, or as part of a special code or language. Its distortion can be taught by one's parents or teachers; distorted communication can be "spoken" at home; distorted communication may be the only medium through which one can gain the desired or necessary response that secures one's survival or gives one needed emotional nutrition.

Distorted communication can be viewed also (although it is a piece of the same fabric above) as being the faulty sending of messages or faulty learning. Reality-based communication consists of correct sending, meaning that the sender conveys what he wants to convey and what he thinks he is conveying. This must be put into the correct code meaning so that the symbols he is using are familiar to and understandable to the intended receiver. The intended hearer must hear the communication correctly; he must hear it as the sender sends it and then he must be able to decode it in the same code the sender uses.

There are opportunities for misunderstanding at every step. The sender may be unable to say (verbally or nonverbally) what he wants to because he is "trained" not to, because he is afraid his "bleat" will go unheard, unheeded, unresponded to, responded to differently than is desired or needed, or he will actually be punished. The sender may be unable to convey what he wants to or needs to because he uses a code that is unknown to the hearer or he has learned different meanings (actual and emotional as in a semantic-differential sense) from those of the hearer. He may have learned a different relationship between communication, action, and consequences, and he may expect his communication to result in a response different from what the hearer understands that he wants and gives. He may also lack communication skill and not know how to say what he wants to say or not even know the reality of what he is conveying through the inflection, tempo, and intensity of his speech, his facial expression and body language.

A hearer can also have similar problems with being unable to hear true meanings, being unable to decode, and lacking the skill to read cues correctly.

Communication not only conveys meaning or content, but it consists also of paracommunication which tells the hearer how the sender wants him to use the message, that is, what he wants the hearer to do with the message. Communication defines the relationship between and among the interactors. The way in which one communicates with another tells the hearer what status the sender thinks he has, what status he thinks the hearer has, the relative power they have vis-à-vis each other, the role prescriptions, the sentiment between them, the norms which govern their relationship, and perhaps also their goals. Distortions in communication can be seen as very crucial in interpersonal relations, as satisfying or as endangering, and as central in the group process.

Distortion in communication can be frustrating to the sender or the hearer and can result in behavior which seems to be grossly deviant. For example, the sender asks for help but uses the wrong code and consequently feels that the intended hearer ignores him or does not care; the hearer fails to hear the intended plea; that is, does not interpret it as such and cannot understand the sender's distress; the self-image of the sender is deflated because the hearer does not validate him. In reality, however, the hearer did not intend to deflate him but the sender conveyed one set of meanings by his words and a contradictory set by his action, both at the same time. The sender sent contradictory metacommunications and created a double-bind; the sender did not convey a message that could produce the desired response; that is, the communication could not achieve the desired goal, and so on. This is not intended to be a complete detailing, but is only illustrative and as such throws light on why teaching communication is so important and also how groupwork can be very helpful in this regard. It also helps to show how faulty communication can explain emotional disturbance, seemingly inappropriate behavior, poor goal achievement, and systems breakdown.

Communication is not only a personal variable but also a group variable. People tend to speak in a meeting in relation to the position they occupy, the status they think they have, their commitment to the group and its goals, and where they think they are in the affectional network.

People communicate as they think their role requires and also in response to a favorable or unfavorable climate which includes such things as trust, sanctions, support, anxiety, and the like.

There is greater communication in a group between persons of similar status, that is, high-status people talk more to high-status people, also high-status people tend to talk more often. People of high status confirm equality by how they address each other, while they talk down to low-status people and thereby confirm their low status. People relate by position and role and thus reaffirm the positions and roles of others, not only by content, but also by paracommunication. People of lower status and positions tend to tell people of higher status what they think they want to hear and in so doing reaffirm and inflate the importance of these high-status people and debase themselves.

89

People tend to communicate more with members of their own subgroups and thereby tighten the ingroup which supports their sense of belonging while those outside of the group are not communicated with and their isolation is confirmed. More often, people who enter subgroups hold similar norms and through communication reaffirm and reinforce these norms which heightens the differences between the ingroup and the outgroup. The communication patterns draw the boundary lines; including some and excluding others.

Communication patterns influence goal-attaining activities by either affirming or denying latent objectives and by negotiating between individual goal orientations and the group goal. Such processes facilitate commitment and hence achieving. It is through communication which defines the relationship between members that power is explicated and this, in turn, regulates control.

There are several major ideas here that must be emphasized:

1. An individual learns to communicate, learns the codes, and learns the relationship between the communication and the consequence through experience with a significant communication network. The group can provide an arena for learning, especially through feedback, awareness, skill-training, and the opportunity to engage in reality-testing.

2. An individual's communication patterns can help him to meet his needs or can thwart him. These patterns can be reinforced in a group by affirming status, role, position, power, adequacy, and belonging by virtue of the communication patterns within the group. On the other hand, the group can provide a "script" which is different from the one the individual (or family) habitually reenacts and by so doing reorient the individual and give reinforcement to new communication options which establish him differently in the system. Such a communication switch can offer new resources, reset relationship alignments, and elicit a new set of behaviors by meeting needs.

3. Communication is the major process through which the individual and his environment transact.

90

In this chapter we approached behavior by indicating that faulty communication may exist in the individual's transmitters, decoders, and receptors. These can be affected through skill-training, awareness, alleviation of anxiety and fear, goal reorientation and similar approaches. Then, I suggested that people communicate in a group by virtue of group structure. In this regard we observe that structural realignments, changes in communication patterns, and feedback can serve to reinforce individual behavior patterns or alter them.

If we put these two ideas together, we can influence the group (treat the system) in order to improve its communication patterns in the service of individual needs. By design, the group will move more readily toward its goal achievement and, more important, it will help the members to communicate so as to maximize their growth and functioning. In this way both the individual and the group are helped.

Group Goal

The word "goal" has been used here several times. In this book "group goal" means an objective (which need not be conscious or explicit) through which each member perceives that if the group achieves the group goal, his individual goals will be implemented in a way they otherwise could not have been. Once again, these two, the individual goal and the group goal, are so interrelated that any change in one results in an alteration in the other or in the system. For example, a change in group goal can cause a member to drop out, to reduce his commitment or participation. to change his behavior to one of conflict or withdrawal, or to perceive the new goal as more responsive to his needs. In all of these transactions, one's behavior in the group is a response to one's needs and hence to the resources in the group and to the group response which does or does not make resources available. The needs variable and the response variable of the individual are, of course, unique to the individual's predispositions based upon genetics, physical and biological imperatives, past experiences, psychological structuring, and cultural prescriptives.

Turning the Construct Upside Down

This is not a book on personality or human behavior although it is a temptation to spell out a
theory of behavior in greater detail. This is a
book on groupwork and the material on behavior is
presented as a framework upon which middle or
practice theory can rest. The human and social
dynamics are offered as illustrations of what
variables are available to practitioners and what
options or strategies might therefore be susceptible of influence. In order to do this, it has
been necessary to attempt to explain how the variables affect each others.

The emphasis in the preceeding pages has been
upon group structure and the social variables.
From time to time, some ways in which group structure influences individual behavior have been indicated. We are going to approach the subject from
the other direction now and briefly illustrate the
influences from the vantage point of the individual. There is the danger that I am laboring the
obvious. I will risk it.

Esteem, self-image, and self-enhancement, are
psychological variables. I am not discussing psychological variables from the structural point of
view, such as id, ego, superego, or as functions,
such as perception. The concepts chosen are on a
lower level of abstraction because I believe one
must move to lower levels of abstraction in order
to be able to relate usefully the concepts to practice.

It has been postulated that behavior is more
directly related to the need for esteem than to
the need for sexual expression[1] and also, that
self-image is an index to emotional well-being.[2]
If one's self-image is high, one chooses goals
commensurate with that image, verbalizes in meetings, expects acceptance and acts to get it, behaves as one who has status, accepts high position

---

[1]Virginia Satir, <u>Conjoint Family Therapy</u>
(Palo Alto: Science and Behavior Books, 1968).

[2]Rogers and Dymond, <u>Psychotherapy and Personality Changes</u>.

with responsibility and risk, and chooses companions who equal and enhance one's image. Esteem reinforces high self-image and gives one a sense of power and control. People with esteem perform better than average, and those without esteem tend to perform below their own potential.

Status, position, and esteemed roles support self-image and self-esteem. Communication is directed to these people so as to increase their information and confirm their esteem; they are sought after and, therefore, they feel they belong. All of these things add up to the conviction that they are adequate, worthwhile, and wanted.

Wish, fear, and anxiety are psychological variables of an order different from self-esteem or self-image, although they are related. It has been postulated that a major aspect of social functioning is the conflict between wishes and fears. Whitaker and Lieberman call this the focal conflict.[1] An individual has wishes which are based upon basic needs but he has learned through life experiences that attempts to satisfy these wishes are fraught with danger. One of the universal wishes in this theoretical formulation is closeness which is to be known, to know another, and to experience, free of fear, a touching of persons. One is constantly wanting and seeking genuine human encounter. In the process of growing up, however, an individual may experience threats, punishments, and rebuffs when reaching out to others. These are devastating to one's self-esteem, self-image, and consequently, to one's willingness to risk interpersonal relations. The hurts may be real or imagined. They may have been occasioned by external rejections or they may have been the product of one's own thoughts, imaginations, or distortions.

Threats, real or imagined, and actual punishments condition an individual to avoid real dangers or anticipated dangers. By association, it is possible to become afraid of persons other than those who are the cause of one's unpleasant experiences and, hence, to raise defenses against people, or certain kinds of people, and certain

---

[1]Whitaker and Lieberman, _Psychotherapy through the Group Process_ (New York: Atherton Press, 1964).

kinds of risks. The kinds of dangers, in addition
to those which lower esteem or fail to validate
one's self, are such things as fear of being con-
sumed or consuming others, fear of being emptied
(such as excavated or of emptying others, fear of
being dismembered or of dismembering others, and
fear of being destroyed or of destroying others.

The group experience in social work with groups
can exacerbate fears or it can support wishes and
give an individual the opportunity and the experience of coming closer to others and finding that
the things which were feared do not happen, or the
individual may be able to learn to cope differently
with his fears than he was able heretofore. One
can learn how to come close without hurting or consuming others. One can learn how to come close
and still prevent others from using one or inviting others to use one. The adjustment mechanisms
become susceptible to more effective cog-wheeling
with external situations through group support,
self-awareness, and learning.

By relating the factors discussed above with
the structural variables, it can be seen that high
position, high status, and power allow one much
more leeway to express and act upon wishes without the increase in or fear of actual punishing
sanction. Low status and vulnerable positions increase fear and most certainly raise anxiety. Communication which leaves one uncertain increases
threat and the chance of being punished and, therefore, increases the likelihood of withdrawal or
garbled responses. Role expectations can provide
supports for wish fulfillments or blocks to such
fulfilling behavior. Moreover, the structure will
allow one to reenact old behaviors or even seduce
one into doing so. One will gravitate to loca-
tions in the structure which "protect" one from
altering behavior and, therefore, one reinforces
one's own maladaptive patterns and repeats them.

Group climate, norms, sociometric patterns,
culture, and decision-making can be effective pro-
tections against certain fears and thereby enable
wish-facilitating behaviors. But the group can be
too reassuring and too anxiety-reducing, thereby
allowing one to retreat and never to learn to cope
with the external realities. One example of this
is that the members of a group of schizophrenics

will relax and fall back into the comfort and
security of old habit patterns unless there is
demand even though these patterns do not meet
their basic needs or fulfill deeply felt wishes.
And so, a group can support pathology and pathological adaptations through its structure and processes or it can enable change.

There are a great many variables in a psychological system as well as many different schools
of thought which employ differing concepts and
words that one could isolate for discussion. Our
purpose here is to show that a groupwork model must
be based upon the interaction and transaction of
system variables rather than upon a more static approach. Modern social work concerns itself with
behavior, especially adaptive and coping behavior.

To adapt means to change to meet conditions,
and to cope means to contend with conditions. However, these are not enough; I must insist that we
add prevention and change to the essentials of social work practice. The psychological variables
from which one might work could be the task orientations of Erikson, such as trust, autonomy, initiative, industry, and identity, or ego functions such
as perception, memory, judgment, intelligence,
reality-testing, postponement of gratification, and
mediation between individual drives and social demands. To these one might add competence, meaning more than the ability to cope or adapt; the
capacity to master the environment.

From the many foregoing illustrations it should
not be difficult to see how trust or mistrust,
autonomy or shame, initiative or guilt, and so
forth can be fostered or to grasp the many ways
in which ego functions are strengthened or blocked
by the position one occupies or the role one plays.
Also, it should seem clear that in any epigenetic
schema the successful negotiation of a stage enables the success of a subsequent stage and prevents the failure of the resolution in that stage
as well as in subsequent ones. If one carries this
a step further, I suggest that the failure to negotiate a stage now leads to a mental dysfunctioning
in later life which is very reminiscent of mistrust, shame, doubt, guilt, ego diffusion and so
on; all of which seems to indicate that there is
a preventative aspect to the successful resolution

95

of the various crises of growth and development.

It would seem reasonable to suggest also that the various ego functions, especially those related to reality-testing and to socialization, are linked absolutely to the opportunities, options, and rewards available by virtue of one's location in the group structure. This would apply as well to the opportunities, options, and rewards that one has to explore, understand, and manipulate the environment so as to change it. To be powerless to alter one's environment or to be helplessly buffeted about by external forces because of one's lack of status, one's lack of power, the demands of a subservient role, or a minority-subgroup affiliation within the group must be comparable to a child's experience as a toddler. In an ongoing study in the Harvard School of Education Preschool Project, Dr. Benton L. White reports that since poor children are often accused of lacking drive for achievement in school, it is very revealing that middle-class children studied spent fifty per cent more of their time constructing things or practicing skills that gave a sense of mastery. One is able to ruin a child's innate ability with an environment where he acquires helplessness. One can also train him to be stupid.

If one has had such experiences, the group can play up one's shame and doubt and immobilize the low-status person, further isolate the isolate; or it can foster independence and allow and promote autonomy. The endorsement of social action as part of social work with groups is essential to the purpose of individual competence and is not a question of ideology.

We must return again to a theme that was mentioned earlier. For most people a lack of structure creates anxiety. People want to know where they stand even if where they stand is not desired by them. They ask for, gravitate to, and seduce others into providing the security of that which is familiar and habitual to them. It is doubtful if the replaying of their script by their enacting their old roles is of service to them. This is a trap that the groupworker (and family group counselor) can be drawn into and which must be avoided; groups very often reinforce inappropriately. Group experience is not necessarily good, or is it helpful to permit a group to "type cast" its members into old roles.

In social work where the purposes are personal development or therapy, a minimum of group structure would be preferred, for many reasons. One is that interpersonal competence is a matter of person-to-person relating rather than structured relationships. It is also preferable to allow an opportunity for considerable interchange of roles, interchange of positions, and a sharing of power. This calls for such concepts as shared leadership, equality, communication of sentiment, freedom of expression for all, differential rankings on many scales depending upon abilities and contributions, decision-making by consensus rather than majority control, and equal access to resources based upon need rather than power. In such a group, status is given for behavior which contributes to the achievement of the group goal and to the enhancement of the members.

To some readers this may sound like unrealistic idealism. The group method in social work is utilized to enhance individuals and to structure the environment to maximize the potential of all. It is a learning ground, a milieu for growth, an environment which can restore, an experience. It should, therefore, be rich in all the nutrients essential to human growth. Dr. Maxwell Jones, the British psychiatrist, once said to social workers in Canada, "a plague on all your groups" because he said they were not psychological human groups but were task groups, fragmented duplications of an alienated society. The social work group is not just any group; it has specific purposes and therefore it should foster these purposes. Most problems which come to social workers are problems of an interpersonal nature. People make people sick or people enable people to be happy and well. Social work groups, therefore, should provide interpersonal experiences conducive to personal enhancement.

After people have been helped to achieve closeness, or as a concomitant, they can learn how to function within a wide variety of structures, roles, and social realities.

The word "therapy" as used above means a pro-

cess that liberates people from inhibiting fears
in a good reliable relationship, frees the ego
potential for creative self-realization, and facilitates the birth of a real self.

Most people grow and live in situations which
are controlled by others and in which they are
submissive to that control. This will be discussed in greater detail later. The social work
group to be helpful must be free of domination.
Growth, creative self-realization, and the birth
of a real self do not occur in an atmosphere of
domination. A typical group usually structures itself so that the members are not free at all but
are locked into role boxes. Many workers make the
mistake of allowing the process to substitute
another kind of domination for worker domination,
as for example, permitting autocratic control to
vest in an indigenous leader, chairman, or a dominant clique. Sometimes the whole group becomes op-
pressive. Domination in any form is still domination.

The Boston University School points out that
a group in the second stage of group development
is concerned with autonomy and freedom.[1] I agree
that true intimacy does not evolve as long as independence from domination is not allowed.

THE AGENCY OR SETTING IS AN INPUT. The discussion has been proceeding around the interaction
of significant variables which influence behavior,
and the group has been the system under examination. In the social work context, the group and
its members function within a larger system,
namely, the agency or setting. Setting is differentiated from agency to mean where the service
is, as in the case of a social service department
in a hospital. The hospital is the agency but the
setting is the social service. Almost all social
work is provided through bureaucratic organization.

The agency or setting deeply conditions the
nature of the service rendered and is the impinging environment of a group where group is the medium
of service. The function and purpose of the agency

---

[1]Garland, Jones, and Kolodny, "A Model for
Stages of Development in Social Work Groups."

set the limits, character, and potential for the service. Though it is often implied rather than expressed, the agency determines the essential essence of the methodology used, such as, whether it is democratic or directive.

In a model where the purpose and method of groupwork are to free the members from inhibiting fears and defensive habit patterns, a bureaucratic, organizational structure with its requirements and procedures can subvert the group process. Decisive consequences may flow from structure and procedures.

In many agencies and settings, there are strains between the function and purpose of the group and social work group methods on the one hand, and latent agency goals, agency policy, agency procedures, and administrative convenience and prescriptions on the other. Many settings provide a milieu for the group which is not congruent with the purpose of the group and even frustrates it. For a group to achieve social work ends there must be organizational support for group services.

The agency influence on the functioning of the group can be approached from several viewpoints. We will examine but a few.

The status afforded the members and the group in the total service will influence group behavior and the behavior of the members. For example, if the group has low status, members will be reluctant to belong, or may develop a strong, exclusive ingroup as a protection against the agency and its administration. The members may have low self-images and nurse feelings of rejection. Such a situation can result in alienation, withdrawal, disaffection, submissive dependency, or covert rebellion. Of even greater consequence is the fact that the group which is given low status will reject the values and norms represented by the agency.

As we have seen, a low-status location in the structure affects the access to information and knowledge. This also can lessen participation, commitment, satisfaction, and the sense of belonging. When these conditions prevail, dropping out or at least a lack of concern is likely, and one can predict deviant behaviors.

For the agency milieu to be conducive to group functioning and to individual growth, it must minimize status differentiation, reduce the sense of powerlessness, reduce the sense of isolation, increase group decision-making, and seek to match the organization's policies, procedures, and rules to the functional needs of the group and its members. Polsky found that groups in an institution for emotionally disturbed children were less likely to need external controls and discipline as opportunities for group decision-making increased, nurturance (need-meeting) became greater, and resources (staff time and attention) were more available.[1]

As a generalization, the greater the frequency and stability of interaction, the less social distance there will be. Social distance increases feelings of isolation, and reduces opportunities for testing realities in social interaction. Social distance increases mistrust. In host settings such as hospitals, schools, and institutions, there must be an atmosphere which permits risk-free testing of reality, love and the receiving of love, and also facilitates self-expression. If the setting does not allow these things, and input into the group engenders fear, then the transaction of the group with its environment is anxiety-inducing. Social distance influences how the group members feel about the agency's importance in their lives, and whether they can regard it as a reference group.

The agency structure tends to be authoritarian and as such is an example of the use of power; it is a training ground in democracy or in manipulation. If the group is perceived as a training ground (especially in youth groups) for democratic living, it must be democratic. If this is not so, the "noise" to use a term from communication theory, drowns out the stated purpose. Noise means all those messages which are the real communications or are "telling it like it is." Group members are sensitive to noise and soon learn to pay greater attention to it than to the stated purposes.

---

[1]Howard Polsky and Daniel S. Claster, <u>Review of the Dynamics of Residential Treatment: A Social System Analysis</u> (Chapel Hill: University of North Carolina Press, 1968).

Noise is especially influential in values,
norms, and goals. Goal displacement in the agency
structure may subvert a goal from helping people
to learn to relate to each other, from helping
them to grow and function more successfully to
such goals as administrative convenience, procedure rigidity for the sake of procedure, staff
comfort, responsiveness to community pressures,
agency self-perpetuation, economy, prestige, or
empire-building. The behavior of the group and
its members will be responsive to their social
context. Groups also have past experiences, predispositions, and group cultures which transact
with the environmental influences. The group focal
conflict always can be resolved in favor of fear
if the agency is repressive, domineering, punitive, or controlling.

As an agency increases in size or structural
complexity, it becomes less and less able to meet
the heterogeneous needs which characterize the
group members because the maintenance of the structure requires a more patterned, stereotyped behavior on the part of its constituents. Therefore,
the bureaucracy of the agency reinforces the bureaucracy of modern living, and dehumanizes the
members which is, of course, the very thing we are
trying to undo.

The more formalized the structure of the agency, as is true of the group itself, the more reli-
ance will be placed on operating rules, frozen-role
structures, staff preoccupation with the internal
workings of the structure itself, and structure for
the sake of structure. As this occurs and increases, there is a disposition to seek techniques,
standardized methods, "scientific approaches to
practice," "disciplined use of self" and emotional
detachment. It becomes difficult, if not unreward-
ing, to provide a good reliable relationship which
can free ego potentials for creative self-realization in such a setting. A real self is afraid to
be born.

The more formalized the agency structure, the
more selectively it will attract certain kinds of
people as staff and as clients. It will attract
people who are less anxious in a structured situation and it will more likely attract middle-class
clients and members. Social workers, by and large,

are relatively more bureaucratic than professional, that is, they carry out agency policies and procedures more often than they use professional guidelines for behavior.[1] Groupwork and bureaucracy are not compatible and social workers who work with groups must be more conscious of the relationship of structure to service. In 1964, it was indicated that of the social caseworkers studied, only one-tenth served their clients as their major frame of reference before thinking of agency, profession, or setting. The one-tenth were also the innovative ones. We have no similar study of group-serving social workers. In the model presented in this book, the social worker must encounter his group members as a person and not as a role-carrying bureaucrat.

Another way of thinking about agency as an input is to look at the ego-strengthening aspects of the agency structure and procedures. A foundation stone for ego functioning is a sense of trust. This implies, in Erikson's terms, to be trusting, trustworthy, capable of trust, and able to trust one's self. The nature of agency structure often seems to be devised to protect against clients and to channel them in prescribed routes which will control their passage through agency process. Some agencies seem not to trust the client and so reinforce the client's lack of being trustworthy. Agencies are not to be trusted when they do not negotiate in good faith.

It is because not all social institutions are trustworthy that we hear social work spoken of as negotiation, mediation, or advocacy. The worker is being enjoined to help the client obtain from the institution what is his right and what the institution professes to be set up to give. The helping relationship must be a "reliable one" and it is difficult for it to be reliable if the agency is not reliable.

Locked rooms, locked closets, patrolled halls, and night guards at camp belie trust. Universities, slowly and reluctantly, are removing the re-

---

[1]Andrew Billingsley, "Bureaucratic and Professional Patterns in Social Case Work," Social Service Review (December, 1964), 400-07.

straints which have characterized college dormitories because such rules do not foster ego strength nor do they reinforce trust. Since trust and hope go together, a failure to enable a sense of trust to be confirmed also denies the prospect of hope.

In actual practice, autonomy is more often denied than is trust. Institutions, schools, and group-serving agencies need to have structures which fully support a sense of independence because a failure to do so leads to a weakening of adequate and potential functioning. Self-discipline, responsibility, and social control are not effectively taught if the encounters are battles of wills in an atmosphere of control and submission. This position is as equally defensible if one prefers learning theory to ego theory. Learning is effected through positive reinforcements, and in this context rewards would be given for independent thinking and acting if the end sought was creative and innovative individuals.

Closely related to the question of autonomy in practice is the establishment of initiative. In a society which prides itself on its creativity and self-motivating values, initiative is a most desirable ingredient. If the purpose of ego functioning is to be fulfilled, initiative must be supported by agency structure. It is regrettable that such is not always the case. In the model which is presented in this book, autonomy and initiative are prerequisites for the capacity for or competence in intimacy, and intimacy is the most important objective being postulated here for social work with groups. Consequently, agency structure must be reorganized so that it can cog-wheel with the group. It is not tenable for the group to be the only place in the agency or setting where the member is encouraged to participate in decision-making, to have initiative, and to be creative; nor is it supportive for the individual to find two contradictory sets of mores, one in the group and the other in the total institution. It is, of course, even worse if the agency blocks what the group culture supports. This seems to be an occasion where the group might be involved in social action.

If the group is to be involved in promoting

agency change and social innovation, the group
needs to develop a structure which will enable it
to withstand opposition without sacrificing its
goals or resorting to self-defeating behavior. Although at first glance this may look like a simple
or obvious statement, it is a most important principle in practice. If it is not developed, internal splintering and conflict evolves, as can be
observed in the current student and civil rights
movements. Essential to its achievement are interpersonal relationships based upon trust rather
than position and role, explicit goals and commitment to them, division of function based upon
skills rather than status and role, status based
upon contribution to goal achievement, leadership
viewed as a function and not as a position, widely
shared and disseminated communication, equal access to resources which means that power exists in
functions rather than in persons, decision-making
by concensus rather than through the power of subgroups, and an allegiance to organizational flexi-
bility, meaning that change and adaptation is built
in instead of stability. Social stability not only
is no longer a "good," it is no longer a reality
in an age of change. Organizations, like orga-
nisms, must be able to adapt to survive.

CHAPTER 4

BUILDING BLOCKS IN CONSTRUCTING A MODEL

The building blocks that will be used in the construction of a working model for groupwork are not original with me. They have been borrowed from many sources and I am indebted to their originators and developers.

Talcott Parsons has had an influence on the formulation of the first proposition in this model; it is he who speaks of psychological, social, and cultural subsystems as being both interdependent and interpenetrating. He sets forth the fundamental beliefs which are the foundation stones for this model. These are stated here in simplified language:

1. All human action is directed toward goals. Whenever a person does something (acts) he is trying to get something done (goals).

2. All human action is rational. It is a function of one's innate needs and orientations. What a person does depends upon what he needs (wants and prefers), how he looks at things, and the position in which he finds himself.

3. All human responses have two stimuli; feeling and thinking.

4. All human action involves a selection between alternative orientations and responses.

5. Selection involves evaluation (standards) of what, to the individual, seems best for him and what others say is the right thing for him to do (norms).

6. All human interaction involves a complementarity of expectation (role reciprocity).

7. There is a lasting pattern to the way people act (modes of adaptation).

8. Groups of people often behave suprisingly like individuals.

105

A social system is a structure of relationships. Behavior is determined, in part, by one's
place in the structure or one's perception of one's
place. Where one is in the structure determines
one's access to resources. Other people place one
in the structure, determine one's roles, status,
and expect behaviors for which they give rewards
or punishments. Rewards are need-meeting and punishments are need-denying. The first proposition
in the model is that behavior is a response to need
and how that need is met gives rise to other kinds
of behavior; the resources that are available to
meet this need are a secondary stimulus to behavior.
Responses can become habitual and, hence, become
modes of adaptation.

A person's position, status, and role determine, in part, what resources will be available to
him and his location determines his behavior by
virtue of the response of the situation to the need-
seeking behavior of the person.

Need orientations are universal but they vary
in dominance from person to person, time to time,
and situation to situation. Persons have predispositions for need and response based upon genetic
factors, physical attributes, past experiences, and
preferences. Some predispositions are innate and
others are learned.

Social experiences can precipitate responses
as they act upon predispositions. If the social experiences are continued and perpetuated, the behaviors are repeated and, thus, one's responses can
become habitual. It can be assumed, then, that
all social behavior is learned. It follows also
that perpetuation occurs through reinforcement.
Reinforcements are rewards that both precipitate
and perpetuate responses. When rewards are both
returns and incentives for primary (basic) needs
or for learned needs they are called "secondary
gains."

It follows also that coping and adapting are
learned and they are learned in the same ways in
which other behaviors are learned. Also, socialization into a culture, that is, conformation to
its norms and expectations, is learned through the
same processes; for example, the need to belong is
acted upon by group pressures and one conforms to

avoid rejection. The need to be liked, to be right, to be validated, to gain favorable response, and so on activate behaviors to achieve these goals in response to the resources available in the group and as one gains rewards (primary and secondary) one learns to perform. This performance may not be in accordance with the expectations of the group or may not meet the individual's basic needs; herein lie distortions, misperceptions, and limitations which can explain discrepancies. In most instances what has been learned can be changed, new learning can take place, the distortions can be modified, and the limitations (or responses to the limitations) can be overcome.

As behaviors are learned and become part of habit patterns, feelings also become habitual due to the recurrence of either rewards or punishments. Anticipated threat, anxiety which can be viewed as worry about punishment or failure to meet needs, and fears, become habitual as do modes of adaptation or responses for dealing with anxiety and fears. Rather than view behavior as a response to the conflict between wishes and fears (which may be theoretically sound), from a practice point of view it is preferable to conceptualize the reaction as habitually thwarted needs and fears which have been learned as one has attempted to reach out to other humans to help meet one's own needs. This idea is neither profound nor original but it does inform practice in a way that other formulations do not.

Selective, adaptive behavior is not a simple response to a force but is made up of responses selected to improve one's chances of reaching goals as the individual's motive[1] system seeks to find ways of reaching goals. It has preferences[2] but it reacts to what is available. The social and environmental systems provide (or deny) opportunities and options. Selective behavior is based upon information about things, about resources, and about the responses of the environment to the individual's need-gratification-seeking behavior. Such information presumes the necessity of a cybernetic system for learning, adapting, and coping. The in-

---

[1]Meaning unconscious motives.

[2]Preferences are consciously made decisions.

dividual must have accurate feedback in order to respond appropriately and in accordance with goal facilitation.

The second proposition in the model is that it is not enough for one to learn to cope and adapt to the environment. Since the environment provides (or denies) the opportunities for need-meeting and the available options, it controls the destiny of the individual except, of course, for the choosing one does within the options. However, all available options may be depriving or, at best, poor fare. Social action is essential as the individual must be able to make the environment more suited to his needs and the needs of others. I wish to go farther than R. H. White who sees this only as a need for the growing infant and to set it forth as a necessity throughout one's entire lifetime.

This is not a social-goals model as perceived by Papell and Rothman. A social-goals model presumes that the desired ultimate is the enhancement of the environment, be it group, neighborhood, or community. My conception is that the environment is a tool, an instrument, or a facility which must be fashioned to serve people. I do not accept the idea that the individual exists for the State, or the social-psychological concept of group qua group, or the social-contract theory which might support the idea of a mediation between society and the individual. The social unit has validity insofar as it fulfills the needs of its members and social action is promoted here in the interest of the individual. This model might be called "the matching model," borrowing Gordon's terminology. Mediation implies a go-between to bring about an agreement between persons or sides. The sides become connected but not directly articulated since they must be connected by some other person or thing. My idea requires that the individual and his impinging environment transact directly; this is the essence of the matching model.

The third proposition is that in addition to coping, adapting, and mastering, mismatching must be prevented as much as possible. Social work in general has been slow to address itself to prevention and its preoccupation with psychoanalytic theory has directed its energies primarily to treatment. More recently, thought has been given to a preventive role for social work with some attention being given to epidemiology. At the same time, a few authors argue that prevention is not feasible in a social context because one never knows whether what one is trying to prevent would not have occurred anyway if one had not been trying to prevent it. This is an intellectual argument which does not appeal to me because I think we know enough to be able to predict probable results from certain kinds of deprivations and impositions. Social work must give far more time and energy to social prevention and to the adaptation of a social health approach from public health practice.

From its inception, social groupwork has been the one specialization in social work which has promoted prevention as a major aspect of its practice. When social groupwork joined the greater social work profession--the number of its practitioners was small when compared with social casework--social groupwork, awed and influenced by social casework, demoted social action and prevention from their places of importance in its theory and practice in order to conform to the therapeutic and corrective stance of the majority specialization. However, social groupwork in its traditional setting has always adhered strongly to its role of prevention which is to the credit of these group service agencies. In the model presented in this book, I reaffirm the premise that prevention is an integral part of the practice of social work with groups.

Prevention means not only the provision of need-meeting nutrients, the elimination of endangering elements, the making available of growth-inducing group experiences, the training of interpersonal skills, and the like but it also means inhibiting deterioration processes and keeping things from getting worse. Social work through group process is method, not policy. Social work with groups as method and process can and does prevent dysfunction. The question of policy is not being discussed here. More will be said about this later.

The forth proposition is that it is the group and the group process which are the effective media for growth and change in the members and, to some extent, in the group's environment. In this model

the social worker is not a change agent as such.
The social worker is part of the group system and,
therefore, is part of the group process but he is
not able to direct the process, or to change people or their behavior as one molds a piece of clay.
The worker has an influence but he is not the influence. Every member of the group directly and
indirectly influences the process whether he acts
or not, and whether he wills it or not. The process unfolds as a consequence of the interaction
of all of the members as each is constantly selecting behavioral options available to him.

The worker influences the process within the
limits of his position, status, role, and function
to the extent that these interact with the psychological dispositions of the members, but the same
must be said of every member in the group. Whatever the worker does or says or refrains from doing or saying, he is but one force among many and
it is the emergent responses of each to each and
each to all which direct the group process. The
group will operate on its own themes, its own conflicts, its own goals, and its own culture with
the worker or in spite of him. It is the group
that is the experience for its members. The worker
is not a group member but he is part of the system
and the processes of the system. He is within the
group boundaries and he carries a specific function
which differs from a member function.

The worker may have knowledge, resources, or
skills which members do not have and which they can
use or not as they choose. Each member also has
knowledge, resources, and skills that the worker
does not have and which the group may need or can
use and which may be vital to another member or to
members. Worker and members are equals as people
and they are partners in a group enterprise. The
function of the worker is unique and is enunciated
in the contract. The function of the worker is to
enable or facilitate the achievement of the purpose
of the group and group members.

The fifth proposition rests upon the fourth,
namely, that the social work group is a system of
mutual aid wherein each member assists every other
member to meet his needs, to create a maximizing
environment, and to achieve the group goal (which
if achieved is perceived by the members as helping

110

each member to achieve personal goals). This concept is not the same as cooperation. In mutual aid, each member is helping the other and is expecting that he will be helped. Since my premise is that favorable response, self-image, recognition, validation, and so forth come from significant others, how else can each be served except by other members? Is the approval of the worker all that one wants or needs? Perhaps the answer to that is in the affirmative in a system based upon domination and control. In such a system the authority figure is all-important because one is in danger of being put down unless one has his approval and recognition. The model presented here seeks to eliminate such a situation and it is the mutuality in the group that provides the most healthful meeting of needs which can result in self-realization. It is in mutual aid that the individual and his environment can be symbiotic and all the resources available in the group can be shared by all.

The temptation is to say, "shared equally," but the needs of each are not equal, and the predispositions of each are not alike. The idea that everyone must be treated alike and receive the same treatment in a group is a fallacy. Mutual aid in this context means that each gets what he needs from the others in the group and gives what is needed by them. It also connotes that each and all are working to improve the system (or situation) so that it will serve better the needs of all. The overall concept, while not at all the same, may be grasped more easily by recalling the graph which demonstrates the dynamic balance of supply and demand in economics. The point at which the two lines meet is the point of operational balance. In this context, the point at which the lines representing individual need-meeting and the need-meeting of others coincides is the most viable operational balance. That point can be raised by such things as improving the system, increasing resources, facilitating the transaction, and reducing the friction in the mesh.

The sixth proposition is that the desire for human closeness is innate and its achievement is essential for health and survival. People need what other people have to offer and it is through others that human needs are met. Healthy growth occurs when human closeness has made need-meeting resources available and enabled the growing person to utilize them. Maladaptive behavior, stunted growth, failure to realize potential, and unhappiness result from a lack of closeness and, in turn, perpetuate the inability to achieve closeness. Anxiety, fear, the inability to risk, distorted communication, and the inability to reach out to others or accept the reaching out of others are related to the punishment experienced and perpetuated when the person had reached out in the past. Ego-function--which includes perception, memory, intelligence, judgment, reality-testing, and self-control--is limited also in growth potential through threats that one experienced in seeking favorable response and validation from significant others.

There is a deep and all-abiding yearning in everyone, unless it has been destroyed by tragic experiences, to mean something to some person or persons and to reciprocate. One wants to appear important in the eyes of others and to know that others care. Everyone wants to feel that it matters to someone whether he lives or dies, is happy or depressed, is pleased or pained and, in turn, everyone wants to be of use and consequence to others. It is important to be missed, and important to have someone who can be missed. The opposite of love is not hate; it is to be ignored. As unpleasant as hate is, it is a relationship that confirms one's being, but to be ignored means that one does not exist. The birth of a real self depends upon the look in the eyes of others, the softness of their touch, and the warmth of their feelings toward one. People learn to love by being loved. They learn to care by being cared for and if one has not had that experience, it is difficult if at all possible to acquire the capacity to be close with people. It is a misuse of words to speak of falling in love. People do not fall in love, they grow into love.

Since learning to care about others is learned through experience, the group must be an experience in mutual caring if it is to fulfill the purpose of helping people to maximize their potential. In any helping relationship, the experience must be congruent with the purpose and so in casework, for example, if the caseworker-client relationship is not one of human closeness, is not an experience in mutual human relationship, it is meaningless. In social work with groups, the group, that is the member-to-member and member-to-worker interactions, must become experiences in closeness and mutual aid. Such an experience is possible if trust has been established and control has been minimized.

Group dynamics has been subjected to study and research by small-group and organization theorists. For example, some schools of social work use Homans almost as a textbook in teaching groupwork.[1] Homans did his research in an industrial plant and used production as a criterion. Much of the small-group research also uses production, either explicitly or implied, as the criterion for success. In the context of this book and in social work, production is not the ultimate good. The very idea that by introducing "human relations" or sensitivity training into groups the production output will be increased has an exploitive ring to it. I am concerned about wasted lives, man's humanity to man, with human potential, and much less with production.

Production has made the United States affluent and powerful; it has not made it great. The people in this country like to think of themselves as kind, and good, and great. The election slogans of the last three administrations have promised a "Good Society," a "Great Society," and a "Just Society." If these societies are being promised, one could assume that they still do not exist. A "Just Society" is not one that creates and perpetuates "White Racism;" a "Great Society" does not use its power and affluence to support forces of reaction in other parts of the world; a "Good Society" is not one characterized by poverty, crime in the street, and the Chicago Democratic Convention. Don Luce and John Sommer make the point in relation to this country's objectives in Viet Nam. They state that we must be able to demonstrate that we understand the people of Viet Nam and are sensitive to their needs. It is their contention that we cannot win hearts or minds through technical virtuosity or production alone. It is essential that we have concern for the human spirit if our policy is

---

[1]George C. Homans, The Human Group (New York: Harcourt Brace & Co., 1950).

to succeed.[1] It is my thesis that the capacity for concern and sensitivity to people's needs must be developed and experienced in the process of growing up and that this is one of the most valuable potentials of the group experience in social work.

Arnold Toynbee, the eminent historian, said, "This choice that is open to us for using our technological virtuosity is not man's only distinctive gift. Besides being makers and users of tools, we are social, moral and spiritual creatures, or, alternatively, anti-social, immoral and diabolical creatures, if we choose death and evil instead of life and good. This aspect of human nature is more important than its technological aspect. At a pinch, we could survive without apparatus, but we could not survive without at least a minimum of good behavior....

"The significance of a landing on the moon lies in its forcing us to face--and, we may hope, to deal effectively with--the ludicrous, but also perilous, discrepancy between our attainments in technology and in morals. This gap is very great and is growing greater day by day. Our generation's task is to try to raise our morals to a level at which they will be spiritually adequate for wielding the enormous power, for either good or evil, that our technological progress has already thrust into our hands."[2]

Groups in schools, institutions, social agencies, churches, and the like must become groups that provide the kind of understanding and responses for which Luce and Sommer ask and the interpersonal morals of which Toynbee speaks. Production is not the be-all and end-all of human existence. If we are to have a good, great, and just society, attention must be given to providing opportunities for such human experiences.

As of now, we are on the brink of an age of

---

[1]Don Luce and John Sommer, Viet Nam: The Unheard Voices (Ithaca: Cornell University Press, 1969).

[2]Arnold Toynbee, Toronto Globe and Mail, July 8, 1969.

leisure in this country. Very soon production and work, especially the kinds that connote drudgery, will be done by machines and we will be catapulted into an era where man can no longer value himself or others by what and how much they produce. Work and production, per se, are fast becoming outmoded criteria. The world we are approaching is going to have to readjust its living to new concepts of value, for the use of time, and for what has meaning.

In a world freed of drudgery and the need to compete on a dog-eat-dog basis, the human individual can find meaning in service to others and in the devotion of time and energy to meet the needs of others. Groups and corporate institutions will be seeking status and favorable response through providing human satisfactions. Yet, our universities are still operating on the work ethic, our schools are models of the Protestant ethic, and our suggested solutions for our poverty-stricken and black population is to train them to know how to work. Social work and groupwork should not evaluate groups by their production or design methods to form groups to produce. It is very important that we begin to understand what living in a leisure society can mean, to develop conceptions of human potential in our thinking, our theories, our system of beliefs, and our practice. A concern for the human spirit is an essential.

I do not doubt their sincerity or impugn their motives, but I wonder whether the strong push for techniques and manipulative-helping methods is not a reaction to the cries of people for closeness and freedom.

The seventh proposition in the model which is presented follows from the preceeding one. Throughout, I have been speaking about domination and submission, about control. In addition to closeness and the deleterious effects of punishing the responses of reaching out to others in order to meet one's needs, but directly related to it, is the thrust to be free. Shulman cites Piaget who points out that there are few opportunities for the growing child to experience self-determination and freedom from control.[1] As this is so for children,

---

[1]Shulman, A Casebook of Social Work with Groups.

perhaps it is even more so for adults in Western
society. The structure of the family is hierarchical with control vested in certain positions and
statuses. The peer group emulates a "pecking order," the public schools are authority systems
which not only discourage individual blossoming
but are frightened to death of it. The simple
truth of the matter is that adults in general and
the established hierarchy in particular are ter-
rified lest people become innovative. There is a
worshipping of equilibrium as a "good," stability
is rationalized, and socialization comes to mean
status quo. It is an assumption to be challenged
that the conforming child is the good child, that
the nonconformist is not quite well, that adjustment means doing what one is told, that one should
not "make waves," "upset apple carts" but should
"grin and bear it." We go so far as to define ego
strength in these cultural terms by suggesting that
a strong ego is one which postpones gratification.

It is my contention that manipulation shuts
out potentials for growth, that creativity does not
develop in authoritarian systems, and that self-
realization is not facilitated when one is being
controlled by others. The model herein calls for
the freeing of individuals from binding controls
so that they can be and become themselves and experience the élan vital of the thrust toward one's
potential.

I am not advocating permissiveness, anarchy,
undisciplined selfishness, or nondirective social
work. In the first place, there is no such thing
as nondirective social work because as long as the
worker takes the stand that the group will be denied any direction, he has already directed it.
Many people have great trouble with these concepts
because their own experiences have been controlled
and they have incorporated and internalized the
"situation" so thoroughly that it is hard to conceive of freedom without equating it with value-
laden words like "permissive" or "chaotic."

It is the nature of systems to seek equilibrium and to resist change. Systems exert energy
to maintain the systems and to coerce the parts to
"stay in their places." Systems like conformists
and, therefore, social systems devise ways and
means of educating and training the well-machined

116

cogs that can function smoothly in the well-oiled machine. Social workers have no business training cogs or supporting the status quo and, hence, groupwork has no call to develop groups which "control" or stifle freedom. The free-wheeling cogs create tension and, therefore, create "trouble" for the system. These considerations have prompted some people to say that a true systems model is inappropriate for group and community work since it promotes tension reduction in the interest of system maintenance (like keeping the summer cool). As a result, the idea of spiralling was introduced to allow for the system to move to reduce internal tension. I suggest that matching is a more viable construct.

Real self-realization is not possible in an atmosphere of control. I like Erikson's terminology when he says that we must learn to want to do what we have to do, but there is a subtle note of manipulation in it and it seems better to me to say that we must learn to want to adapt to what cannot be changed but also to know when it can be changed, to want to change it, and also to be able to change it. Such change is not a spiral which implies an unknown momentum, but is change with a goal orientation, the goal being matching.

Freedom is a frightening concept and while we yearn to be free, we are anxious and fearful of having to make our own decisions and to live by them. It requires more energy, more investment, more ability, and greater maturity to think for one's self. If the decision proves to be a poor one, we have no one to blame. So it is that groups want chairmen to run things, clients want workers to tell them what to do, and most students want to go to class and be lectured to. While that is what they want, their spirits rebel and they feel infantilized, molded, demeaned, and angry. They want and accept the situation because they have learned to be comfortable while under restraint. They have been trained to mouth democratic slogans but to fear freedom. A very small percentage of students are resisting now and are struggling for freedom from inhibiting control.

Since the assumption is that domination frustrates growth, that domination is one reason why people are unable to achieve closeness, and that domination is a source of anxiety and fear because someone with power has all the resources needed for survival and can use that power to grant or withhold them, therefore, no form of social treatment can be effective in a structure of control. If the relationship of the helping person to the person being helped is one in which the worker believes he controls or in fact does control, or the person being helped conceives that he is controlled, there is no effective growth-promoting helping going on. The allegation that casework is ineffective is not true if one means the method; what is true is that social workers are ineffective when they push people around. This is predicated on the statement that only one-tenth of the workers studied were responsive to their clients while nine-tenths held as their first allegiences their profession or the bureaucracy. Mullen's studies,[1] as well as those done in psychology, would seem to indicate that the acts of the helping persons studied fall into five classifications, the five classifications presuming to be the essential ingredients of the method, and that the acts called supporting and responding appear significantly less often than those which are questioning, confronting, and advising.

No similar studies to my knowledge have been conducted in groupwork except for a small exercise which rated groupwork students in field work in the School of Social Work at Ann Arbor. That study indicated that those groupwork students were weak in their use of the group process.

It seems unreasonable to evaluate democracy as a failure when as yet we have not tried it in this country any more than we have practiced Christian religious teaching. The same applies to casework and groupwork. It is unreasonable to evaluate them when they have not been properly utilized. I hypothesize, as an example, that in Girls at Vocational High the "casework method" did not designate what precise methods were used nor did it explicate the question of control and authority. One is led to believe that the girls were

---

[1]Edward J. Mullen, "Casework Communication," Social Casework (November, 1968), 546-51.

118

not disposed to use casework help.[1] Moreover, it would seem that the impinging environment, that is, the Vocational High setting, is hierarchical and the girls were subject to a dominating faculty and administration. This being so, the input infuses the relationship with domination. A careful examination of the facts, it seems, would also reveal metacommunication telling the girls who was boss in the so-called helping relationship. The writers of that study must have been well aware of this. More will be said about such research later.

To digress for a moment, social workers are under attack by the welfare-rights groups who accuse them of not being helpful and of perpetuating poverty. By way of a weak defense, social workers really cannot free their clients as long as they work in settings predicated on domination and submission. However, one cannot defend social workers' submission in such settings.

The elimination of control, to the extent possible, calls upon the members of a group to learn to use themselves appropriately within the agreed-upon contract of mutual aid for the achievement of personal goals within a milieu that is conducive (through negotiation) to the fulfillment of the other members. The worker is not the controlling agent because self-regulation takes place in a negotiation among members and an attempt is made to balance "supply and demand." The worker, at least in the initial stages, acts to make the members aware of what is happening in the negotiation, gives support to their efforts, and seeks to use himself in the interest of all of the members in their enterprise.

Once the members agree, in contract, to the proposition that the group exists to maximize each and all, then the worker, who is their agent, supports this end and helps them achieve their goals. This is not permissiveness, it is quite the contrary. The focus is on what the members want and on a working out of the balance of one-for-all and

---

[1] H. Meyer, E. Borgatta, and W. Jones, _Girls at Vocational High: An Experiment in Social Work Intervention_ (New York: Russell Sage Foundation, 1965).

all-for-one. The safeguards that keep this from
being anarchy, chaos, and permissiveness are the
dynamic goal of effecting a matching and the worker
working with and for the members to that end. This
makes him a partner, not a boss.

For there to be freedom, there must be choices
available. Helping the group and the members to
explore alternatives, establish options, and make
choices is an important key in the method. It is
only by having options that one can be self-determining, and the engaging in an exploration of the
consequences of chosen behaviors in each option effects movement toward goals. Such social work attests to a belief in the dignity of man and a respect for his rights and integrity.

This discussion, however, is not about decision-
making in the usual sense and it has little to do
with formal procedures, motions, votes, and formalized agreements. In some groups, discussion may
be quite logical and cognitive, but the behavioral
options even so may not be consciously thought out.
Feelings may be verbalized, felt, or only vaguely
sensed, and yet may be most influential in the making of choices among options. In most instances,
the underlying dynamics leading to goal selection
means that selection and choices will not be cognitive or even conscious. The bulk of the process
will be nonverbal, with emotional communication and
metacommunication. The worker must be sensitive
and skilled in keeping track of what is going on
and in being able to decode the real negotiations
that are taking place. However, unlike the members, he will often verbalize the interactions,
feed back the communications, and respond to the
meanings and feelings within the group. Social
groupworkers tend to respond to overt content and
they must learn that the real work of the group
does not go on at this level.

Along with choice must go responsibility so
that the group members are confronted with the ultimate in freedom, namely, that each man is responsible to himself and for himself and that he cannot
escape by blaming others. We are in many ways responsible for how others act toward us and we are
in a position to change their responses by changing our actions, or the situation. This is a very
important concept and can be experienced through a

change of script, role playing, and other programming as well as the ongoing group interactions. Feedback can be most helpful in these processes.

The eighth proposition leads from the seventh, namely, if the members are responsible and free, what are they going to do about it? "It" refers to whatever is the group's concern or task, and whatever are the goals of the members. It is their responsibility to do something about it, they are free to do something, and they have other people to help them. This proposition brings the model into the here-and-now. What is the group going to do to resolve its concerns now? What has happened to them in the past is too bad. It is important to know about it, to study it, to understand it, and to accept it as the fact of the matter so as to reinforce or extinguish, build in supports, neutralize fears, and so on, but the past is not to be allowed to justify the status quo, or to excuse current malappropriate behaviors. The present structure of position, status, or role, may be a contributing cause and it can be changed. The individual's perceptions or feelings may contribute also but these can be changed. The question to be put to the members is always, "What are we going to do about it now?" as they explore options, alternative courses and means, and as they negotiate with the impinging environment. (The worker is not negotiating, the members are.)

This leads to the ninth proposition which involves actions and the probable consequences of possible courses of action. In this proposition, and in the discussions of choices and responsibility, freedom, negotiation, and control, the important learning is not primarily cognitive, that is, not intellectual. In the literature, much is made of awareness and insight in therapy. Standing alone, awareness is not a motivator for change. Awareness plus a clearly known and understood goal begins to create a readiness for change. The significant factor in the group process is the addition of an experience to the other two. The concept here, to put it in sequence, is that the members must be helped to bring forward their concerns, feelings, and individual goals first, and then, to become aware of their goal-achieving or problem-solving behavior. The behavior or action is examined and evaluated to ascertain whether it, in fact, is congruent with the goals sought. This pursuit is carried out in the present life experience in the group and is clarified through the eyes, ears, and feelings of the other members. It need not occur through words and word meanings but may come about through interactions in program such as games, activity-planning, or a sharing of feelings which are acknowledged through motoric stances, gestures, or body language. The worker can, and often does, openly express what has taken place.

It is possible now, in an atmosphere of trust, free of domination and committed to mutual aid, for alternative courses of behavior to be tried and for consequences to be tested. One of the greatest assets in working with the group process is that one can test what probable consequences might accrue from certain actions for reaching specified goals. The action can be altered and new behaviors learned as a result of this experience in an environment which is reasonably safe, with a worker who can be relied upon and trusted to protect the learners from hurting themselves, hurting each other, or hurting him.

However, there are prices to be paid for actions and whether the gains achieved or anticipated are worth the price is a decision which the members alone must make for themselves. Prices come in different forms, such as postponement of gratification, comfort, change of habit, self-esteem, renunciation of secondary gains, pain, effort, and so forth. The members may not know the prices and may have to be helped to find out the probable costs, or they may have no idea that alternatives exist for them. Some may sense that there are alternatives but lack any hope of their successful achievement. With help and allies, the possibility seems more attainable. It is probable that hope will come more easily from a successful venture in the group than from just talking about it.

Still another positive lies in the group becoming more sophisticated in its ability to "map" or size up a situation and find the alternatives. It is fashionable and professional to hold that the worker diagnoses the situation, then selects the point of intervention, the strategy and, by assessing leverage, applies the force. Why is this the prerogative of the worker? Part of the action, especially as it relates to social change, can be assessed by the group, as previously stated, in partnership with the worker.

The Mechanics of the Model

While this book is not meant to deal with how to do it, it is necessary to discuss some aspects of how the model works.

Techniques are not important and cannot be relied upon in working with groups for social work objectives. There are only a few techniques in social work and these have been stated and restated in the literature by each writer as though he had found something new. They can be worded to sound like discoveries or reworked into many formats, but essentially, they are similar in all of the helping professions. They fall into three main categories; support, awareness, and learning. They may be important to learn from the point of view of study and theory, but there is no bag of tricks or kit for working with a group. The worker is unable to control all of the inputs in the group's operation because the members, the environment, and the culture are feeding into the interactions and transactions at all times. The intra- and intersystem action is much too complicated and rapid for the worker to be able to analyze immediately all the data so as to make conscious and specific professional interventions into the group process with considered, immediate goals in mind. When the worker is engaged with a group, each member is feeding in stimuli along with the group entity, the setting, the events just past, the impinging neighborhood environment, invisible committees, and so on ad infinitum. Each member as well as the group are responding. The worker would have to be like a computer doing complex factor analysis to be able to react in a split second with a calculated intervention supposedly chosen to effect a particular result.

In a real sense, the worker is a computer and he is making rapid-fire decisions in response to the data that is being fed into him (and from within him), but he is not able nor is it feasible for him to make interventions, act by act, to effect specified results. The worker is not the change agent; the group is the medium for change. However, the

worker is part of the system and his behavior is
an influence depending upon the many factors of
structure, group stage, psychological predispositions, and the like.

The worker operates from a stance. He cannot
hope to be effective on the basis of specific interventions or acts per se. The worker must be
clear in his own mind about his stance as well as
comfortable with it. He must know his own function, his goals, what he believes, and who he is.
To the extent possible, he should also know about
his own predispositions and modes of adaptation.
Moreover, the worker ought to be aware of his feelings and be able to express them appropriately.
The worker is a poor example if he is unable or unwilling to express anger, hostility, anxiety, fear,
as well as love and concern. Why should the members be expected to express their feelings if the
worker cannot or will not express his? How can the
members experience an appropriate handling of feelings if the worker is unable or unwilling to handle
his own human feelings?

This point of view is different from that held
by many competent authorities. Nonetheless, I am
proposing that it is useful for the worker to be
able to say, for example, "I am feeling quite anxious because of your attack on me" or "Such disregard for others makes me angry at you." Many children and adults are emotionally upset because they
have learned (been taught) that it is unsafe to
express feelings and, therefore, they have no out-
let for them. If the worker cannot express or accept feelings he is reinforcing the prohibition.
If the members are restrained from expressing feelings, they are not having an experience in learning
how to handle them.

When a worker in a group meeting is intent
upon analyzing the process so as to make conscious
interventions, the chances are excellent that he is
not hearing what is going on and that he is oblivious to the feelings of the group, the members,
and to their concerns. It is of the greatest importance that the worker be responsive to the en-
treaties of the members. To do this he must be
free to listen and to hear the messages that are
imbedded in their communications. The more the
worker is engaged in an intellectual analysis of

the events and persons, the less he listens and hears the group process.

The worker must be comfortable about his stance; that is, he must agree with it philosophically, he must believe in it and have confidence in his ability to help the members achieve their goals. A variety of studies seem to confirm these factors as being indispensable in the helping endeavor.[1] It seems clear that the worker must know who and what he is and what he believes so that his behavior will flow naturally therefrom and, also, so that he will be free from conflict.

There is no question about it, the worker reveals himself to the members through his para- and metacommunication and no matter what he says or how he says it, the message comes through. If he feels punitive his statements will be punishing, if he thinks domination he will be dominating, if he feels superior he will convey superiority. If the worker uses the model proposed here but does not believe in it, the model will be ineffective in his practice.

On the other hand, if he is committed to meeting the needs of others, if he believes in the equality of members and worker, if he is convinced about self-determination, and if he is comfortable with freedom for himself and others, his stance will elicit responses commensurate with it. If he likes the members, they will know it but if he thinks of them as little monsters they will know this too, be they children or board members.

It is because of the messages in the communication as well as the noise that techniques are unimportant. If the worker sees himself as a helping person and respects the members' right to their goals, his acts will flow from his stance and he will be responsive. Consequently, he must see his function as enabling the group process, as helping the members accomplish what they can within the limits of the well-being of each and all, and of

---

[1]Charles B. Truax, "Significant Developments in Psychotherapy Research," in Progress in Clinical Psychology, ed. by Abt and Riess (New York: Grune & Stratton, Inc., 1964).

freeing the group. He must view himself as a partner in the group enterprise.

In the past, it was believed that the worker should not meet his own needs in the group. This is patently nonsense. Let us say that he should not meet his needs at the expense of the members and the group. Little has been written about the meaning of the therapeutic experience for the therapist or of the group experience for the social worker. The experience must affect the worker if there is any validity to the thesis of this book. The worker can and should grow as a direct result of his involvement with the members. He is part of the system and he is a partner in the enterprise. If the group is engaged in mutual aid, the worker is included.

The worker is environmental to each member as well as being within the boundary of the group. The worker in this model does not handle situations, make people do things, or manipulate factors. The worker handles himself, that is the only thing he can handle; he is the only person he can make do anything because the decision to act always lies within the actor. By handling himself, he can affect some aspects of the environment of others and by being responsive he can provide resources that might be needed or used by others. The worker and his behavior are part of the reality.

He is not a mediator between systems unless the members are unable to mediate. Preferably, he helps the members and the group to mediate. He is not a negotiator for them either unless they are unable to negotiate. He helps the group and the members to negotiate. He is not an advocate for the members but he helps the members to advocate on their own behalf. He may advocate with them, but not for them. However, and this is the important point in these last paragraphs, he is <u>their</u> man. His function is unequivocally to help them achieve their goals within the context of matching. This was not the purpose in <u>Girls at Vocational High</u>, nor is it in most agencies. Trecker's old concept that the worker is a representative of the agency is no longer a viable concept.[1] This is a

---

[1]Harleigh Trecker, <u>Social Group Work</u> (New York: Whiteside, Inc., 1955).

new era, and there is a different conception of helping. We are helping the members to be and become, not helping the agency to mold them.

This concept creates many problems with some agencies and administrations. Some have always given lip service to self-determination and democracy but really have not believed in it. Some of the problems are obvious, such as the worker is paid by the agency and the agency calls the tune; the board makes the policy and the worker must execute it; and the agency represents the organized community and it wants to socialize its members (social control). It creates problems for the ideological agency which has a purpose and the right to fulfill its purpose. The most vexing problem comes when the members aim to change the agency or community which is paying the worker. It has been said before that social agencies should be committed to change and have built-in mechanisms to facilitate change in function, procedures, and policies so as to keep in tune with the needs of the members and the times. Organizations tend to stabilize and to resist change. However, the social worker should be dedicated to change. The entire system for the delivery of social work services is in need of an overhaul. However, this book is not about policy or social work institutions; it is about method.

There is also a hidden factor which is that professional workers often are not comfortable in that function and do not accept it. If we are in agreement on the freedom proposition in this model, then the worker can be the servant only of the group and its members. The contract contains the proviso that what is maximizing for the members must also match the maximization for others; the entire premise is within the context of self-realization and growth. This enjoins us from securing firearms and eliminating anyone we do not like. Also, it has been pointed out that within the group experience there is learning about the relationship of goals, actions, and consequences.

The worker is not a mediator or negotiator for the members or the group unless they are unable to perform these functions for themselves. He can be and often is a liaison and in that function he can explain and interpret the extrasystem, he can act as a communication bridge, or in some instances he can act as a linkage as, for example, when he is the only point at which the two systems can transact in order to attempt to match.

He is, of course, a role model but so are the members models for each other, depending upon position, status, power, norms, and the ability to meet the needs of others. Should the worker become significant in the lives of the members, they may emulate him and should he become a "fink" in their eyes, they may reject his values. If he demonstrates that he is genuine and is their man, the probability is that some or all will learn about interpersonal relations and appropriate behavior from him. Then they may learn the meaning of closeness from experiencing it and also find that many of their fears are unconfirmed; they may experience honesty, learn how to express and deal with feelings, and learn about respect. If the worker is to be such a role model, one concludes that he has learned to trust others as well as himself, he has successfully negotiated autonomy so that he can be independent and allow independence with no need to control others; he must have achieved purpose through initiative and be secure in his identity. Having hope within himself, he can hope that the members will grow and gain confidence through sensing his vision of what is possible.

Strupp and Bergin have become convinced, they say, that the therapy of the future will consist of a set of specific techniques which can be differentially applied under specifiable conditions to specific problems, symptoms, and cases.[1] This may be so, but our knowledge up to now does not make this possible and, until it does, the approach that is suggested here seems to be the most effective one we have. The socio-behavioral, learning theory, operant approaches do seem to change behavior but to the best of my knowledge we have no evidence that they promote self-realization or the birth of the real self.

Strupp and Bergin are correct, no doubt, inso-

---

[1]Hans H. Strupp and Allen E. Bergin, "Some Empirical and Conceptual Bases for Coordinated Research in Psychotherapy, etc.," _International Journal of Psychiatry_ (February, 1969).

far as one can assume the importance of a differential approach, that is, some groups sometimes need more structure than others, or more demand made upon them to get to work. The characteristics of the worker may be an important variable and some groups at certain times may need more authority or control than others. The developmental stages in a group's life require different worker stances. We may at some later date know more about the kind of worker that is most effective with a particular group having a specified set of tasks. As of now, when I speak of being responsive, I mean that the worker is flexible enough to respond to the needs of the members and the group within a range of acceptability. It is axiomatic that the worker responds differentially to each member depending upon the member's need. This is natural and normal for a social worker.

The word "enable" in groupwork came into disrepute a few years ago because some authors thought it was mealymouthed, weak, and lacking in goal. These writers, like Strupp and Bergin, are looking for techniques that can be specific to particular behaviors and can make it possible to designate which buttons to push, levers to pull, and which identifiable target areas to hit. The word enable can connote a lack of goal but it need not. If I can find out what you want to achieve, help you to recognize why you are not succeeding in achieving it, help you to eliminate the blocks and to develop skills, then I am enabling you to move toward your goals. The strength and the power lies within you. The model in this book is predicated on the belief that strength lies in the members and in the group, and that social work builds upon the strength of the members.

I am aware that analogies are imperfect and illustrations often misfire, but in the interest of clarity I will try to define and refine the concept of enabling. When the engineers built the tunnels at Niagara and diverted the water so that it dropped hundreds of feet and hit the fins of the turbines, they harnessed the power of the river and directed it. Some schools of thought in groupwork use this approach; this is not our model. When physicists found a way to unlock the energy of the atom, they freed its power and then they could direct it. In our model we free the power and let the group direct it.

It is my assumption that much of the power in the members and in the group is locked up and inhibited and that other forces may be misdirected. The members and group are enabled through unlocking this power.

The major function of the worker and the main concept in this model is to free the members. One could say "free them up." This means such things as free them from inhibitions, free them from old conflicts and the residues of old conflicts (mistrust, shame, guilt, doubt, anxiety, fear, and so forth), free them from the effects of previous domination (fighting against father and mother figures, transferences, rebellion) and from current domination, so that they can be themselves. It means to provide an opportunity for a freedom of choice among reasonable options with support and encouragement to risk making choices. It means the explication of and clarification of goals, the examination of the assumptions underlying these goals, the beliefs they hold, and the contradictions that have been compartmentalized.

This requirement of the model is the most difficult for the worker and the members. For them, freedom of choice is frightening and risky, and they find it difficult to believe that they have that freedom or that they can trust the worker or themselves. Why should they believe it when each time it has been promised they have been deceived by parents, teachers, friends, and employers? "Feasible citizen participation" was promised by the anti-poverty program but was soon withdrawn when citizens' groups began to exercise choice. Up until recently, students have been given the impression that they could make choices affecting their lives and were admitted to the conference table only to find that faculties did not intend to negotiate in good faith. It turned out to be a procedure used by them only to convince the students that the faculty decisions were right. Organizations, government, universities, institutions, student councils, and social agencies have used the trappings of democratic structure to give the illusion of free choice and, therefore, people do not trust the agency or the worker when he professes to give them their right to decide for themselves.

130

It is difficult also for the worker because he is beset by anxiety lest the choices they make turn out to be "wrong." Unless they can make some wrong choices they will never learn the consequences of certain acts. Such learning occurs only through experience. The problem in the American culture is, partially, that adults do not trust their children and professionals do not really trust clients. Due to our schooling and the way our political institutions operate, Americans do not really learn to believe in and trust democracy. The potential for education for democratic living lies in social work through group process, especially in the group services agency, and it also needs to be freed.

It seems to be difficult for Americans to let go of their children, their students, or their subordinates. Perhaps the reason is that Americans do not experience freedom and, therefore, are unable to know how to give it. Some readers will deny this vigorously and say that American parents have been guilty of permissiveness. Some poorly-advised columnists are blaming campus unrest upon the alleged permissive behavior of parents just after the Second World War. This can be dealt with best by quoting the dialogue of children in a club group.

First child: "I have to go now, my mother wants me home by nine o'clock."

Second child: "If I come home late my father gives me what for."

Third child: "My parents don't care when I come home."

Emotionally illiterate observers would say that the parents of the third child are permissive, but the message is in the words "don't care." The bright hope would be that a fourth child could say, "I don't think I should stay out any later because I have to get up early to go to school. My parents and I have talked about this and they feel that I have sense enough to come home at a reasonable time."

The campus revolt is against domination but, even more, it is against hypocrisy and deceit; the deceit of not caring masquerading as permissiveness

and domination concealed in the structure of democratic processes. Also, what appears to be permissiveness may stem from a reaction formation to extreme control or conflict and from ambivalence
around domination-submission.

For this latter reason, the worker must be
fully committed to freedom or the members will react
to his uncertainty with the symptoms of anxiety or
anger. It can be expected, in any event, that the
members will test his sincerity and conviction.
This predictable probing tries the best of workers
and even the most skilled may be seduced into a
position of authority. If this does happen, the
members become convinced that the worker cannot be
trusted; that it is a ploy, as usual; and that the
worker and members are playing the old game; that
is, both know that really there is no free choice
but they act as though there were. The worker must
not allow himself to be caught in this trap and he
can prevent it by controlling himself and feeding
back to the members what is happening.

In this model, it is mandatory that the worker
face the group members with the realization that
they are free to make decisions which affect them
in the group and that they cannot blame anyone but
themselves for failing to achieve the maximum within the situation. Unlike many adaptations of psychological theory, the members have no recourse to
blaming objects in their past. They cannot excuse
themselves because of their mothers, or their fathers, or fate. They are being asked to take responsibility and are being helped to see that they
will have no one to blame but themselves if they
do nothing to change the situation. The question
is, "What are they going to do about it now?"

There are those who are willing to take the
blame for their own condition and who may even
revel in a masochistic orgy of self-flagellation.
The choice lies with them to decide how best their
needs or preferences can be met once they have an
awareness of the pleasure they gain from suffering.
At this time, the member must be honest about his
goals and what he really wants; the pleasure of his
pain or a change. In this revelation he can make
a choice and has at his disposal the mutual aid of
his fellow group members and the worker. They,
the members and the worker, have the resources of

practical support (advice, counsel, help with environmental situations), emotional support (sympathy, encouragement, companionship, recreation, acceptance, respect, love), and educational reorientation through presenting reality and providing relearning experiences through enforcing and extinguishing.

All of these resources are in the here-and-now and exist in abundance in the group. These resources in the group exceed by many times those available in a one-to-one encounter.

The model prescribes that the worker be himself and that he not be role playing. It asks the worker to encounter the members as a human being who wants to help them and who is ready, willing, and able to perform a function (not a role) as himself. I am asking the worker to divest himself of his uniform, his insignia of position, and his obeisance to the establishment. If he cannot meet his members without these indicia of office, he really is not free to engage in an interpersonal relationship. If he cannot be himself how can he expect the members to interact as themselves? If he needs the protection, the guidelines, and the facade of structure, they will have to cling to these fictions also. To avoid a semantic misunderstanding, let me restate the position: I am asking the worker to perform, as himself, the role that is appropriate to the function and not to role play. This might be illustrated by the case of a social worker who at five o'clock takes off his social work uniform and becomes a different person in his interpersonal relations, attitudes, and way of life. What he is as a person will come through if he role plays and he will stand revealed in his "emperor's clothes."

The more "professional" social workers have become the more they have become concerned chiefly with things involving the intellect, the more "emperor's clothes" they have donned the more they have alienated their clients. The professional role has been used to hide the absence of the human being within. These are the significant variables that are ignored by social researchers.

Field instruction experiences in many schools of social work are enforcing and perpetuating the development of this kind of worker, one whose head is full of "facts and theories" but whose being is empty. Social work education in the field tends to emphasize content and technique.

Lest some reviewer accuse me of attacking social work, I am not impugning social work. I am committed to social work method and believe that it is effective and of great service to humanity when it is utilized properly by suitable people. When carried out properly, social work is an experience in closeness.

The social worker in this model realizes the importance of interaction specifically designed to achieve closeness and trust and to demonstrate the worker's commitment to human relations based upon honesty, respect, and dignity.

The group experience is a "slice of life." The members are "playing for real and for keeps" with a real worker; the group experience is reality.

A viable group is one which is working on its concerns and in which each member is free so that he too can be working on his concerns. This does not mean pathology, and it does not imply therapy. It is normal and natural to have concerns about the problems of daily living, interpersonal relations, growing up, and the usual crises of the developmental stages. The impingement of the environment and its demands make for concerns. The worker must be able to hear what the members are concerned about, receive their messages, and be responsive. Shulman has been helpful and also explicit about how these concerns are educed.[1] In what he calls the "offering stage" he tells us that the worker "tunes in" by studying the group and its members, much of which can be done prior to the group's formation, through an analysis of age, sex, culture, and other face-sheet data. The worker "listens" at the meetings and by the hints, leakage, actions, assignment of roles, and symbolic communication of the members he tries to get the meanings of their behavior. He also utilizes his

---

[1]Lawrence Shulman, "The Anatomy of the Helping Act," paper at the National Conference of Social Work, New York, June, 1969.

knowledge of communication blockages which hide or distort meanings and tries to elaborate on the communications and to interpret them while eliciting and inviting an expression of feelings. The main purposes of the worker in this stage of the endeavor are to look for and facilitate the emergence of affect and to help the group place its concerns on the agenda. It is very easy to do exactly the opposite by being too active, too studied, too program-directing, and too interrogating. It is more important for the worker to be sensitive and to listen and hear.

The following quotation sums up this section. It was written by a psychiatrist but not about emotionally disturbed people in treatment and it is applicable to the context in which this book is written, social work through group process.

"In general, the leader's role is that of picking up the predominant feeling, or its lack; noticing when the group seems especially aroused about a subject, and wondering about the cause; attempting to bring the more withdrawn members into the discussion; and attempting to separate himself from an authoritarian or teaching role. Intermittently, the group will use the leader as an authority and occasionally the requested information is offered, if it is not felt that it will block further movement by the group. However, the leader's role is primarily viewed as directed toward facilitating and stimulating emotional communication among the group members."[1]

The model being presented is applicable to all practice where the frame of reference and objectives are those of social work. For example, it is recommended for groups in institutions, work with mothers in aid to dependent children and families, parents of emotionally disturbed children, retarded children, physically-handicapped children, and for groups of retardates, the emotionally disturbed, and the handicapped. It is applicable to child-guidance clinics, schools, juvenile courts, child-welfare settings as well as rehabilitation

---

[1]Louis S. Cholden, _A Psychiatrist Works with Blindness_ (New York: American Foundation for the Blind, 1967), p. 39.

centers and medical centers. It will be effective
in public social services, in private family agencies, and it is suited to family group counseling.
This list is not exhaustive but is only illustrative.

A section further on in the book is devoted
to the group services agencies. This model is advocated for those traditional agencies such as
settlements, community centers, Y's, church groups,
the B'nai B'rith, Young Judea, and so on. It is
not designed as a model for groups that are primarily task groups such as committees, boards of
trustees, and decision-making groups where the decision or group production takes precedence over
the growth and development of the people involved.
It is strongly advised for block and neighborhood
clubs, enhancement groups in community-action programs, anti-poverty groups, and, in general, in
the underdeveloped areas in the community because
these are the groups of people who need the kind
of group experiences that will help them to develop ego strengths, social-action skills, self-
respect, and will be compensatory for the deprivations to which they have been subjected by a punitive and ungiving society.

CHAPTER 5

SCHEMA FOR DIAGNOSING GROUP FUNCTIONING

There are many articles on diagnosis of individuals and of individual behavior but few on
group functioning. For the same reasons that one
needs to be able to assess individual behavior, a
schema for assessing group behavior would be valuable.

The following typology would be much neater
were it in chart form, as it is before me as I
write, but, unfortunately, the production of this
book does not make it feasible to reproduce a
large chart. I will attempt to set it forth in
outline form and hope that it will be useful to
the reader.

The nine categories listed are the main classifications into which group functioning may be
divided. In a good theoretical typology the categories do not overlap; they are mutually exclusive. This one is not presented as a scientific
classification schema but rather as an aid to the
social worker in practice; besides, people are so
inconsistent and perverse that they do not fit
easily into neat boxes or labels.

The paragraphs which follow each category
elaborate on the dimensions of the category and
give some of the indications that may be manifested
in the group behavior. The symptom picture cannot
be precise because the actors are evidencing modes
of behavior that are unique to them in response to
reactions to general-feeling states such as anxiety,
threat, frustration, fear, and unmet needs, or to
such general states as mistrust, shame, doubt,
guilt, role diffusion, and the like. The cause of
these feelings can be multiple, or can be attrib-
utable to many aspects of the interpersonal relations, structure, and mismatching. Equifinality
is a system (group) concept that makes it impossible
to isolate any simple system or cause-and-effect
relationship.

I. __Where the Problem Lies within the Individuals:__

    A. Where the individuals in the group are so

needful that they are unable to function
in a group, are injurious to others, are
in conflict within themselves:

1. Individuals cannot communicate or do
   not respond appropriately.
2. Individuals act out and their bizarre,
   seductive, ego-alien behavior is
   frightening to others.
3. Individuals control the group by virtue of nuisance value, fear, or contagion.
4. Behavior is withdrawn, apathetic,
   isolated, or fearful.
5. Members exacerbate problems of others.
6. Group supports pathology or reinforces
   symptoms.

Indications: Acting out, bizarre behavior,
extreme provocation, distorted communication,
withdrawn behavior, fear, etc.

B. Where individuals have no interest in the
   purpose or goal:

1. There is lack of cohesion.
2. There is lack of commitment.
3. There is lack of any group goal, contract, or agreed-upon goal, or where
   goals of the members are contra-
   indicated for each other, or for the
   group goal and purpose.

Indications: Exploitation, apathy, conflict,
scapegoating, do not listen to each other,
ideas attacked before they are expressed, intolerance, no movement toward developing or
working toward goals, etc.

C. Where the grouping is inappropriate:

1. The role behaviors set up an isolate
   at either end of the range of accepted
   behaviors.
2. The individual symptoms cannot be tol-
   erated by the group.
3. The group composition is out of balance
   with group purposes.
4. The group composition is out of balance,
   that is, the composition is weighted

138

on the side of negative rather than
positive factors and toward pathology
instead of health; when taken as a
whole its fulcrum is not at a modal
point but skewed so that the negatives
outweigh the positives.
5. The grouping is not suited to the
psycho-social level of tasks, needs,
and resources.
6. The members have primary allegiance
to reference groups external to this
group.

Indications: Reinforcement for existing behavior, anxiety about revealing self or sharing, absence of mutual aid, mistrust, punishing each other, absence of bond, etc.

D. Where individuals have personal value conflicts.

E. Where individuals have excessive super-
ego controls.

II. Where the Group Is in Conflict with the Environment:

A. The environment superimposes demands.

B. The demand of the environment is excessive.

C. The structure of the environmental system
is inadequate or inappropriate to carry its
function, as for example, it is frustrating,
rigid, and punitive for the group.

D. The values of the group are in conflict
with those of its environment.

E. The group does not understand the demand.

F. The group is unable to fill the demand.

G. The group leadership is anti-social.

H. The group is rejected by the environment.

I. The group is in conflict with authority
such as worker, agency, subculture, community, culture of society.

J. The environment is noxious, endangering, seductive, anomic, or contradictory.

K. The environment does not provide access to resources that are needed by the group and its members.

L. The kind, nature, and intensity of the relationship of the group to its environment is inappropriately dependent, nonstimulating, overprotective, seductive, overly stimulating, overly demanding, defiant, exploitive:

    1. The agency's values, procedures, and culture are contrary to the group's and the agency superimposes.
    2. The neighborhood is hostile to the group and its members.
    3. The forces of social control are hostile to the group and its members.
    4. The members are impoverished economically and culturally.
    5. The social values in the impinging society are inconsistent and rewards are given for deviant behavior.
    6. The group leader is from reform school or local gang.
    7. Worker is too different from members to be able to accept them, or they him.
    8. The group lacks skills necessary to match the environment.
    9. The group does not want to match environment and environment does not want to change.

Indications: Group solidarity and hostility to anything that is not of the group, antisocial acting out, low self-image, braggadocio, subvention, arguing inconsequential points, autocratic leadership, bullying, scapegoating, projection, rationalizing, ridicule, sadism, brutality, insecurity, etc.

III. Where the Internal Structure of the Group Is not Appropriate or Is Inoperative:

A. The structure is inadequate to meet the needs of the members.

B. The structure is insufficient to carry out

tasks.

C. The structure is too formal, too ritualistic, or too much for the purpose, size, and functioning of the group.

D. The formal structure does not function.

E. The structure is in contradiction to the values of the group.

F. The structure is in contradiction to the group goals or there are no goals.

G. The structure blocks interpersonal interaction or group transaction.

H. The structure works against group movement:

    1. Leadership is too strong, too weak, inept, inappropriate, absent, centralized, there is conflict for leadership, leadership is inappropriate for stage of group development, leadership denies access to resources and thwarts need-meeting, leadership operates through power, power is not distributed.

    Indications: Attendance falls off, dropouts, participation index low, scapegoating, fighting, communication patterns centralized, poor movement toward goals, overstructured rituals and procedures, goal displacement, poor esprit de corps and low hedonic tone, high level of frustration, aggressive behavior, apathy and projection, informal channels wide open and formal channels neglected, taking sides with no compromises, etc.

    2. Positions occupied or available do not meet needs of group or group members. Positions do not articulate or fit each other or the group. The formal positions do not match the informal functioning. Positions and status do not match. Status is not given for performing group requirements. Position and status are unfilled or in contention. Positions and status

block person-to-person interaction.

Indications: Attendance fluctuates, poor
interest in elections, positions unfilled
or poorly carried, clique formation, conflict, inability to make group decisions
or to keep those made, poor organization,
and avoidance of communication channels,
etc.

3. Communication is limited to few, or
   is skewed, is distorted, is lacking,
   is not heard or decoded, is double-
   bind, is not responded to, is not appropriate to desired goal, is delu-
   sional and not related to reality.

Indications: Poor participation, i.e.,
many do not talk, cross talk, talking all
at once, responses inappropriate to what
was said, movement diffuse and in all
directions, schizoid behavior, unreal
communication, group decisions made too
quickly, etc.

4. Role patterns do not meet needs of individuals or of the group. There are
   role gaps; roles are inappropriate to
   purposes, task, or stage; are threatening or anxiety-producing to occupant; not complementary or reciprocal;
   ambiguous; conflicting; overlapping;
   nonfunctional; stereotyped; role patterns block person-to-person interaction.

Indications: Flight, fight, pairing, dependency, acting out, withdrawing, role
playing, inappropriate role performance,
difficulty in making group decisions, escape to irrelevancies and high-level ab-
stractions, silences, hostility, anxiety,
inappropriate reciprocal role relationships, etc.

5. The group procedures are faulty. They
   are too rigid, inappropriate, ritualistic, not followed, inconsistent,
   unformed or unknown, unsuited to group
   purpose or task, inappropriate to

142

group values. Group procedures block person-to-person interaction or consensus. Procedures allow majority to dominate minority.

Indications: Excessive procedures and frustration, insufficient procedures and frustration, wrangling about procedures, undemocratic controls, floundering, impatience, dropping out, poor participation, goal displacement onto procedures and rituals, scapegoating, endless debate with no decision, decisions reached with too little or irrelevant discussion, railroading, etc.

6. Sociometric (affectional) ties are scarce and weak, skewed patterns, subgroup cleavage, few linkages, isolates, rejection.

Indications: Low cohesion, fighting, racial or ethnic intolerance, poor morale, diffusion of group goal, do not listen to each other, ridicule, diversity of interests, difficulty with program, each pushes own plan, idea possessiveness, do not help one another, no hedonic tone, do not share, group breaks under pressure or crisis, denial of access to resources, isolates, no closeness, interpersonal fear, etc.

7. Structure is designed to perpetuate domination, rigid decisions, keep clique in power, monopolize, thwart change, rationalize behaviors.

Indications: "Big Joes" and slaves, nondemocratic decisions, ingroup top clique, communication star pattern, domination, favoritism, power struggles, procedures ignored, punishment and fines, main concern is to gain status, subtle attacks on leadership, obeisance, contagion, physical force, etc.

8. The structure maximizes loyalty to outside reference groups.
9. The structure is a defense against interpersonal confrontation and a re-

sponse to anxiety.

IV. Where the Group Was Reasonably Well Grouped but the Group Composition Is out of Balance:

A. Because of group stage.

B. Because the purpose has changed.

C. Because individual behavior changes.

D. Because a member is absent, dropped or added.

Indications: Unusual acting out and withdrawal, reversal of decisions already made, realignments, attacks on leadership, discuss breaking up, unusual scapegoating, etc.

V. Where the Group Is Reasonably Well Grouped and the Structure Is Adequate for Normal Functioning but there Is a Temporary Loss of Good Group Functioning:

A. There is a new, largely externally caused problem which is causing stress.

B. There is a group crisis.

Indications: Projection, tight ingroup, exclusion, fighting, delinquency, momentary loss of interest, self-discipline fails, reject limits, regression, etc.

VI. Where the Group Is Reasonably Well Grouped, the Structure Is Adequate for Normal Functioning, but there Is Regression:

A. There is a change in the power structure.

B. There is a change in the leadership.

Indications: Conflict and infighting, seek to seduce worker to intervene, suspicion, childish behavior, random behavior, confusion, etc.

VII. Where the Group Is Reasonably Well Grouped for the Purposes, the Structure Is Adequate, but the Worker Does not Promote Good Group Functioning:

144

A. Worker is not sufficiently skilled.

B. Worker is not tolerant.

C. Worker dominates the group.

D. Worker lacks conviction.

E. Worker does not listen and cannot understand.

F. Worker is not responsive and does not enable.

Indications: Fight authority, neurotic transference, retreat, conformity, gross defiance and discipline problems, hurt each other, submission, no movement, etc.

VIII. Where the Group Is Reasonably Well Grouped, the Structure Is Adequate but the Program Fails:

A. Does not meet the interest or needs.

B. Exacerbates problems of individuals or the group.

Indications: Apathy, heightened unrest and disinterest, aggressive behavior, destruction, regression, pathology, scapegoating, chaos, etc.

IX. Where the Group Is Internally in Conflict over Values, Norms, and Standards, Is Ambivalent, or in Transition.

Indications: Conflict, infighting, low cohesion, warring subgroups, poor decision-making, derision, low esprit de corps, vacillation, no group goal or commitment, etc.

Some of the behaviors which are listed above may be viewed, if one is judgmental, as deviant. A more useful way of looking at it is to see that behavior is a response and in most instances as such may be rational and appropriate. The behaviors also give a clue to the developmental stage of the group and therefore help the worker to adjust his stance to the immediate needs of the group in its struggle to become a viable group.

It is to be expected that group members will be wary of closeness in the initial stage and will register all of the behaviors which are associated with testing, or that a group will be seeking to resolve authority and control in its second stage. What is expected and is, therefore, normal in one stage may be a sign of malfunction or system tension that is not to be expected if it occurs in another stage. That which is observed may be quite predictable in one cultural setting, or for a particular age group, or for people in an institution, and be unusual when noted in another setting.

The purpose for which the categories, their dimensions, and the indications have been spelled out is to allow a practitioner to work back from observed responses to an assessment of probable reasons. These reasons then can be fed back into the group so that the members can know what is going on and can make such corrections as they wish; or, if it is the agency or the worker that is the immediate cause of the behavioral shifts, they may make the appropriate changes. The worker may wish to alter his own behavior so that it is responsive to the group and its members.

It is of immense importance for the worker and for the group, if possible, to be able to diagnose the group's functioning in the current interaction and transaction so as to be able to improve the relationships, eliminate obstacles, and more effectively achieve goals. A group (or a family) cannot improve its function without self-awareness and one cannot understand group functioning by compiling individual diagnoses and histories.

The identification and analysis of how the group is functioning is the major utility of diagnosis. The dynamics of the group members' interaction and transactions are exposed for observation by all. Tension, stress and strain, and conflict provide the group members with the opportunity of altering the dynamics or altering the structure. The process of change is a process of tension reduction. The feedback or confrontation of the tensions reflect on the problems of adjustment, of adaptation, or the impinging environment. The psycho-social diagnoses and histories in agency practice would be more useful if the primary emphasis were on interaction and transaction in the here-and-now of group functioning.

Agency practice would be improved if history-taking were focused on explaining present inter-personal behavior. To do so, in fact, requires starting with how people interact instead of starting with a history of the past and working toward an impression of the present. Many individual behaviors which are thought to be pathological might turn out to be reasonable, rational, and necessary for survival, as long as the environmental factors remain the same--these include other people, the script, and the functioning of the system. Diagnosis should start from actual current behavior, feelings, and accurate observations of interaction. The schema for diagnosing group functioning which has been presented here should prove helpful in tracing individual behaviors to group functioning and thereby to assist in helping groups to become more effective in the service of individuals. The purpose of the group determines the relative importance of the factors which have been discussed here.

CHAPTER 6

NOTES ON FIELD PRACTICE

In an earlier part of this book, brief mention was made of field instruction with a promise that we would return to the subject. Different conceptions of practice call for different approaches to education and training. I believe that field work should be designed to provide experiences that will prepare the learner for practice. We are concerned with what he knows, how he feels, what his attitudes are, and what he is. I am consciously not including skills in the usual sense of the term even though many educators assume that the major objective of field work is to train skills.

In the model presented, the essence of helping does not lie in techniques. Most anyone can acquire techniques but as such, in and of themselves, they are ineffective. To become a social worker requires special experiences, while techniques can be learned in many ways, at many times, and in many places. Techniques are a matter of style and workers function differently, developing styles that are suited to them.[1] To have any meaning, techniques must flow from the worker's identity and stance. Field practice should not attempt to teach techniques, but should allow or facilitate workers to acquire techniques in keeping with their identity and stance.

It follows then that through field work the learner should be helped to clarify his identity for himself as a person and as a worker. This is a matter of self-awareness as well as of facing one's self, making decisions about one's self, and learning to be comfortable with both the decisions and one's self. Subtle, but powerful forces in this process are identification with and incorporation of the supervisor or instructor. The stance of this person will leave irreversible marks on the

---

[1]Edward J. Mullen, "Differences in Worker Style in Casework," <u>Social Casework</u> (June, 1969), 347-53.

being of his protégé. These marks may influence
the learner to seek to emulate his teacher, or to
reject his brand of social work out-of-hand. The
kind of demonstration, relationship, and stance of
the field teacher is crucial.

In agency practice, whether or not the agency
retains its junior staff members, has success in
attracting volunteers, part-time employees, and
summer career trainees into social work with
groups will depend almost entirely upon the demonstration of the supervisor (and other staff) in
the relationship with the trainee. The classroom
teacher also reveals whether he believes in the
tenets of social work philosophy in the way in
which he conducts his classes and relates to his
students, but it is the field instructor who turns
the worker on or away.

The learner must be encouraged to examine his
beliefs and attitudes, to find the compatibilities
between them and his feelings and between them and
his behavior. Knowledge can be acquired through
reading, class discussion, and experience, but the
important learning comes from the exposure of assumptions and confronting them. Students can be
free to become if they have the opportunity to expose all that lies beneath the "knowledge," if
they can be permitted to test the consequences of
options to which the knowledge points, and be encouraged to challenge the basic fundamentals of
the whole system of social work and social welfare.

The corollary is that the learner must be led
to a similar exercise about himself and his functioning; that is, in education he must be asked to
carefully dig back, layer by layer, and expose to
his own scrutiny his basic, bottom assumptions.
The question is not are they right or wrong. One
is concerned with whether they are consistent or
contradictory and how they jibe with verbalizations,
feelings, and actions. The tasks are to search out
who and what one really is, to evaluate for one's
self whether it is what one thought one was and
what one wants to be, and the slow, hard process
of becoming.

This process is only in small part cognitive.
The significant aspect of this self-awareness lies
in the experience that accompanies the self-

discovery. The field work experience is the vehicle which brings one's assumptions into focus and translates them from cognitive learning into "gut learning." What the neophyte is growing into is his function and stance as a social worker.

Social work has alleged for a long time that it builds on strength and supports and elaborates on the competencies of the client or member. It tends, however, to develop its diagnostic process and its diagnoses by identifying weakness and pathology which it seeks to alleviate. The model in this book operates on the assumption that group members have the strength to grow and to change. This must be the premise upon which field practice operates.

The learner must discover himself and develop his stance for himself; and that stance is a posture which incorporates his strength, a strength which has been exercised, reinforced, and buttressed through a new and encouraging familiarity with one's self. Thomas Wolfe, in the frontispiece of "Look Homeward Angel," speaks of people catching a glimpse of themselves through the corners of their eyes in the shop window as they hurry by and seeing there, in the reflection, a stranger. In field work the learner stops, looks, and gets acquainted with himself.

There is an obvious parallel between what must happen to the learner and what has been presented as the social-work-through-group-process model. The propositions that make up the model must be honored and applied in learning how to be a social worker.

The field practice enables the learner to face himself, and it is not encumbent upon the field instructor or the school (or agency) to judge, to expose, to elaborate on weakness, to build on anxiety and fear, or to castrate in the rationalization that this is how people learn. It is the learner and only the learner who compares his ideal, his real self, and what he thinks he is, and who seeks the road to becoming what he can and wants to become. This can happen and does happen only if the field instructor provides an experience that enables it to happen.

In order for one to learn to be a social

150

worker, field practice must be an experience. If you have to ask the meaning of the propositions in this book, you will never know. They must be experienced.

A viable medium for learning to become a social worker with groups is a group of students or learners, popularly called "group supervision," but for a model such as the one we are presenting, the word "supervision" has a jarring ring. Supervision has been defined in our literature as a process through which a person who knows more teaches a person who knows less how to do something, or in the administrative sense, seeing that people do their jobs properly. The idea being offered here instead is that field instruction be through group process.

At once the idea presents itself that this is not the only "instruction" we must provide because surely the student will need some individual "supervision" and there are things which cannot be handled or discussed in a group. Our casework colleagues have sold us this belief for many years and I am no longer willing to buy it. In the first place, we have maintained that groupwork is an effective means for helping people to grow, and that it is a strategy of choice for rehabilitation, correction, and restoration. We have also proven that it has powerful supports in peer relationships that do not obtain in a one-to-one relationship, and that it can mitigate against the effects of control and authority vested in a worker. Since most of the problems which come to social work are interpersonal, it is the logical medium for improving interpersonal competence, and it is a life space, that is, it is a here-and-now in which the action occurs and can be examined.

In the second place, this book is antagonistic to dogma in any form. There is no one way to work with people. No one has demonstrated yet that any one method works, works better, always works, or is the only one that works. Consequently, the idea is being offered that the experience of being a group member with a social worker as its enabler is viable and, therefore, that it be a medium for field instruction. If the worker thinks a learner needs some individual attention, or if he does not know how to help the group help him, or he thinks the group is unable or unready to help at that time, let him provide the supplementation of the one-to-one. I suggest that the group experience be the primary medium for developing social workers who are competent to work with groups.

In the third place, group treatment seems to be in vogue at this time, and in all of the helping professions the group seems to be or is becoming a major treatment strategy.

It is suggested, then, that field instruction be conducted through group process, and it is contended that it is essential for the learner to have the experience of being helped through the process that he is there to learn.

The experience must be one of closeness in which students learn (psychic learning) the meaning, feeling, and pleasure of closeness. Many students will have to overcome their anxiety and fear of closeness and loosen their rigidity and uptightness. They must be able to touch others and be touched (psychic) if they are to enable others and, therefore, they must be able to reveal themselves. Many students leave school not only unwilling to be known but looking down upon clients who share their feelings with a worker. Society does not need or want social workers who have not achieved intimacy and who cannot establish psychic contact with others.

The learning in the group of learners proceeds on the basis of mutual aid. The students care and will provide each other with rich and rewarding fare if they are given a chance and if they are not afraid. The all-abiding feeling in field work is fear, and it is reinforced in many schools, in training programs, and especially in field work. Since the most important learnings have to do with self, beliefs, assumptions, identity, attitudes, and the like, the group members have much to offer each other. They also offer support, validation, and favorable response. It is axiomatic that one learns and, in this instance, grows when one's basic needs are responded to and when ego recognition is present.

Growth and learning, especially about one's self, cannot occur unless the learners are free of

152

controls and relieved of domination. But more to the point is the fact that a student cannot possibly learn to allow others to be free if he has not had the experience of freeing and freedom as well as knowing how the member is feeling while it is happening. Can the client possibly know the meaning of being free with a worker who holds all the aces? Can the client know the meaning of an interpersonal relationship or love with a social worker who is not loving and who is just doing a job? The student cannot learn anything about how to allow people to be and to become with a field instructor who judges, dominates, represents authority, and who needs learners in order to validate his own superiority.

A student must be respected if he is to respect his members, and he must be allowed to be and to become responsible if he can ever help his members to become responsible.

The stance of the field instructor is crucial. If he believes that his function is to pour knowledge down the throats of his students; to point out their mistakes; to mold them; to impose values, techniques, and methods on them; to remind them that he is their superior; they will probably become as noxious as he. However, they may have the strength and good sense to help him grow and change, they may submit and remain unchanged, or they may explode. Let us hope that they will educate him through mutual aid and closeness.

When we discussed the use of the model with the group, it was suggested that the worker and members were equals with differing resources and functions. The same applies to the instructor and student and, although they are partners in a joint venture, the purpose of the venture differs from that of the social work group. The group members are learning how to be mature, self-directing people; this is true of the student also, but the student is there to learn how to be a social worker through group process. This is, more precisely, an educational objective. The student must be a person, but now a special kind of person who can help and enable others.

In an educational enterprise, the instructor and student together are seeking knowledge, awareness, and effective helping methods. Not only should the instructor help the student to discover, but he should also be searching for new approaches, insights, and solutions. He should also be consciously working to improve himself as a helping person.

In social work, as in most involvement with people who are engaged in solving problems, there is no one way to do things nor is there one solution to a problem of living. It is not the function of the instructor to lead the students to the way. It is his function to work with the students to discover a way by seeking and selecting from alternatives and options. If the instructor knows how he would approach the problem, it is not his place to tell the students to do it his way. As quoted earlier, Dr. Cholden says, "Intermittently the group will use the leader as an authority and occasionally the requested information is offered, if it is not felt that it will block further movement by the group."[1] This is applicable in the use of a group of students as a vehicle for learning. There will be many alternate ideas profered by the students in the group and the consequences of each proposed behavior will be decided upon and evaluated.

The fact of the matter is that the instructor does not know what to do, or what he would do if he were the student. The student in a particular group is a unique entity in a unique group system and he must find out what he can and will do. As teachers, we have been passing along information as "the truth" which we have acquired out of our own unique experiences (often in the distant past) or out of articles and books. The "truth" lies in the situation at hand and must be arrived at independently. We would know a great deal more about how to help people in groups if we were discovering with our students instead of proposing to teach them what we think we know.

In spite of all that our scientific friends say, at this point in time we are operating on a system of assumptions and beliefs. Each student must find out what he believes and search out the applicability of his assumptions in helping others to reach their goals. This is the major purpose

---

[1]Cholden, _A Psychiatrist Works with Blindness._

of field practice. In so doing, the body of knowledge will be increased and beliefs will be tested and refined for use.

There are bodies of knowledge about people, groups, and culture. It is vital that students acquire knowledge about individual dynamics and that the knowledge be more than reading about it and listening to lectures. For work with groups, it is essential that workers know about group process and this knowledge is difficult to acquire from words or even from experience if the experience is not analyzed and made explicit. The dynamics of group process is learned effectively by observing, experiencing, and analyzing groups wherein one is a member at one time, an observer at another time, and at still another time a worker or co-worker. Field practice should provide the three experiences and a group of students is the logical place in which to begin to observe one's own functioning, and also to learn about it through the eyes, ears, and feelings of others.

One needs to know how groups function without a worker, with a worker, and with different kinds of workers. In a sense, field practice with groups should be an ongoing research effort. As such, it should also probe into the dynamics of the agency and the neighborhood as these are significant inputs and also are legitimate points of entry. We are involved in "matching" and one aspect of matching concerns the group and its impinging environment.

It follows that social action is an integral part of the field experience as a means of learning how to affect the environment but it is also an experience in mastery, the feeling of mastery of the subject matter and the educational setting itself. Social work educators should enable their students to engage actively in social change, in their client groups, in the environment of their clients, and in their own educational environment. Students should be encouraged to influence their classes, their field instruction units, the school, and the university. In this presentation, it is indefensible to deny that the impinging environment of the students must match the individuals for there to be maximization of the purposes of social work education.

155

Faculty members should be delighted when students engage in efforts at social change within the school and be concerned when they do not. When they do not, it may be a symptom of oppression and fear, or at the least, a failure of enabling. Faculty members who cannot tolerate social action directed at the educational system itself, and perhaps at themselves, ought to retire gracefully. The good society, great society, or just society cannot evolve in the old restrictive molds. We must be free, all of us, to challenge the old assumptions and to correct the contradictions that bind and endanger us.

Field practice, then, is more than dealing with what goes on in the group. It has to do with all of the subsystems that influence the members and, therefore, experiences must be provided in a variety of systems. If this cannot be afforded in one agency, several settings should be utilized simultaneously.

It has been a perennial problem to integrate classroom content with field practice. Schools have used many devices to accomplish this end and they have been tenuous at best. These two aspects of social work education should dovetail. In social groupwork there have been serious gaps between them and more often than not what students are learning in the classroom is not in evidence in the field placement.

I suggest that the classroom for social work practice theory be moved to the agency and taught by one and the same instructor who will utilize the actual placements for class content. In this way the instructor can "cross ruff" back and forth between theory and practice. In this way also, both instructor and student can test the application of theory to practice, and can explore to find solutions to problems of practice.

I do not mean "apprentice training," "vocational training," or "clinical rounds." I propose that the formal class sessions be conducted separately from the group field instruction sessions. This also removes the necessity of using the classroom for "experiental training" which is a dubious practice at best. I am suggesting that we replace that slender and rickety footbridge between theory and practice with an articulation of the two so that there also one can achieve a matching.

At this point a reader or reviewer may be feeling that this section is redundant and that the general propositions are being repeated unnecessarily. I could argue that the impact is strengthened by repetition or that the composition is developed by variations on the themes. Such indeed would be the case but, also, I am aware that it is possible for a reader to agree with and accept the propositions and model for working with client groups and to fail to see their application to field instruction. It is possible for some to accept the model and to presume that it can be taught to students through the old methods. It is also possible that one can accept the model intellectually yet fail to conceive that freedom and responsibility are also the inherent rights of students of social work.

The propositions have been presented here in the interest of clarity and in the hope that we will affirm that students are human beings and treat them accordingly.

Group Recording

There is a need to update group recording. It purports to be an account of the group process and also of the social work or helping process. The important and significant things which happen in a group are multiple, complex, interrelated, and psychic. Descriptive recording glosses over the surface; narrative recording sets forth a sequence which appears to reflect what does happen, but much of what happens does not occur in the sequence in which it seems to appear. The narrative group record usually fails to record the most important dynamics and transactions.

The traditional group record reproduces some dialogue, and singles out some of the worker's acts with implications of cause and effect, stimulus and responses. However, the worker's influence in the group is related to how he feels, what he believes about people and especially the people in the group, how he perceives his function, and how the members perceive each other and the worker. The cumulative effect of these aspects are influenced by the group culture and by the larger system, that is, the environment that provides input and feedback for the group. That these factors are significant and that we have always given them credence is agreed, but the group record has not always reflected them.

The record should be an accurate account of the cognitive process in social work; it should follow the worker's theoretical thinking and reveal an analysis of the interaction. Its purpose is to chart the course so that group and worker can know where they are in reference to where they want to go, where they came from, how what is happening is happening, and how facilitating or blocking the process has been. The charting serves as a medium for self-correcting mechanisms in the group and it should be a continual diagnosis or analysis of group functioning.

Records which currently are called process records are not records of systems process; they neglect large sectors of the action, often are monolithic, and do not record the interrelationship and interpenetration of the determining variables. To correspond to a model of practice such as mine, the group record must be a systems analysis record. The objectives and dynamics must be explicit, the variables that are significant at the time must be explicated and their interaction delineated. Such a record need not follow the sequence of overt events but will trace the systems-functioning. It will include assumptions and beliefs, sentiment and feelings, objectives, norms, functions, reinforcements, controls, rewards, resources, needs, games and defenses, adaptations, and so forth. It must accurately analyze communication with its para- and meta-components. It must analyze the worker's function, stance, and behavior; behavior is a much broader concept as used here than acts.

The record must register input which includes agency, impinging environment of school, occupational setting, family, and the like. It must reflect transaction, that is, the interaction of these inputs and their meanings with the individuals, the group, and the worker.

Growth and adaptation do not result from the experiences of one meeting. The stance of the worker and each member, over a period of time in interaction with other variables, slowly and imperceptibly build until at long last one can perceive some results. The careful dissection of one meeting usually will not reveal the factors which build or destroy. The superimposition of the examination of each meeting on previous ones will not reveal them either. These events have little meaning when viewed in isolation and contribute to an understanding of process only when put into a systems framework.

It is conceded that a careful examination of each meeting is a sounding as well as a check on the helping process. Each meeting will begin to reveal movement or lack of movement and will give clues that help to identify the significant variables. Each meeting does indeed have the potential for influencing group members in relation to the group purposes. However, the events are too small to tell much about systems processes and the traditional group process record usually fails to relate the events in a way that informs the understanding or the helping process. It is too circumscribed.

The social work student is usually cautioned to be wary of inferences; he is to record facts and his interpretations. I am very much interested in what the worker is inferring, how he feels about the events and people, how he thinks, and how he perceives himself. The worker will know few facts about the group members; almost everything he observes is infused with his inferences. His inferences and his responses are correlates of who and what he is, his self-image, and his stance. These inputs must be in the record because they explain him as a component in the system and give meaning to his functioning.

The record should reflect the worker's sensitivity, his beliefs, his attitudes, and his understanding. It is not what he said that matters but what he meant; what was wished or feared; how it was given or withheld. We need to know what was reinforced, reactivated, suppressed, or educed. These factors are indispensable if one is to understand the group dynamics and they can be understood primarily through inference. The kinds of inferences the worker will make and how he will respond depends upon what he knows, but also upon what he is. Group analysis is largely a matter of inferring.

We must develop and teach a new kind of group recording, one that will be appropriate to our latest conceptions of practice. The record should reflect a continual systems analysis. As such it is a record of dynamics which sets forth the interaction and transaction of all of the pertinent variables within the boundary of the group and the impinging environment.

CHAPTER 7

THE GROUP SERVICES AGENCY

Since about 1949 there has been growing disaffection between traditional group services agencies and social work--more specifically, social
groupwork. It is alleged that what is taught in
schools of social work is not useful to the agencies or wanted by them; also, that graduates are
unable to fulfill the expectations of the agencies
which employ them. In the early fifties, social
groupwork theoretitians began to invest social
groupwork with therapeutic characteristics. Treatment is regarded by agency personnel as connoting
pathology and traditional agencies do not presume
to be therapeutic in that sense. Historically,
they have been developmental, cultural, attitudinal, and ideological.

Social casework grew out of the background of
the friendly visitor who came to help the family
with its problems while group services agencies
grew out of a history of companionship, communion,
and neighborly mutuality. These historical differences have influenced greatly the self-image of
the two services and have left their imprint upon
them.

While groupwork as a method struggled to develop a theoretical frame of reference, it veered
sharply in the direction of restoration and, by so
doing, created a greater cleavage between theory
and practice.

The trend in social casework, in the therapies
and in social welfare, has now begun to shift its
focus to concepts of coping, adaptation, short-term
treatment, reality therapy, here-and-now, existential therapy, learning theory, socio-behavioral
rather than psychoanalytical theory, prevention,
systems theory, and family group counseling. One
finds new terminology in social casework such as
mediating, negotiating, expediting, facilitating,
linking, advocating, and the like. In effect, the
movement is toward what had been the position of
social groupwork in the past, not only in the way
in which caseworkers use groups but in casework

per se. Moreover, more are using groups in the groupwork tradition instead of acting as poor imitators of psychologists or psychiatrists working with groups. Parenthetically, many psychiatrists are now leading groups and writing about them like social groupworkers, that is, for purposes of socialization, growth and development, and interpersonal competence instead of for the restructuring of personality or the affording of insights. With the exception of the brilliant work of Schwartz, most groupwork teaching is plowing along in the rut that casework furrowed years ago or is becoming more manipulative.

Through these developments, the traditional agencies have remained aloof, not trusting theoretical groupwork or the schools of social work. Most of these agencies, I suspect, are unaware of the changes in social casework and social work in general and by virtue of the "gap theory" have espoused group dynamics, sensitivity training, encounter groups, and community development, but are still rejecting social groupwork.

In the early sixties, one academician presented a paper at a national conference in which he said that because there were relatively few groupwork master's degree graduates available, it would be more provident to employ groupwork in therapeutic settings than in group services agencies. The implication was that traditional agencies did not use social groupwork appropriately because they did not direct their services to the restoration of specific dysfunctions. It seemed that group services agencies were being eased out of the social work circle and, by like token, developmental objectives and prevention were being relegated to a lower status and, therefore, were unworthy of the attention of social workers with masters' degrees.

The use of groupwork in group services agencies is a matter of policy and it is hardly appropriate for faculties of schools to make policy for social agencies. It is not proper either for academicians to assign objectives to a method. These prerogatives are strictly for agency people and more suited to decisions by those seeking the services.

The prime questions are whether social group-

162

work is a method which can effectively serve the purposes of the social agency and whether it is congruent with the basic philosophy of the agency. Within a range of options, is social work through group process a method which agencies choose to use, implying that it is, in their opinion, an efficient and effective way to help their members achieve their goals? As late as 1969, at the National Conference of Social Work in New York City, there was a session on the question of whether groupwork is an appropriate method for the group-serving agency.

It is a fundamental premise of the model here that social work through group process is a means of helping people to grow, develop, and maximize to their full potentials. The method is useful in enabling people to self-realization, identity, and the birth of a real self. These objectives are reachable through meeting the basic needs for validation, favorable response, support, and above all, closeness. Groups can be systems of mutual aid and through group process people can learn to enable others and, in so doing, can also find themselves. These seem to me to be the functions of most group services agencies.

I have affirmed that social work through group process is suited to a developmental epigenetic frame of reference and that through group association people can acquire, stage by stage, the experiences which support trust, independence, purpose, industry, and identity. They can also learn the expected behaviors for each age, sex, social situation, and cultural milieu. People exercise and strengthen ego functioning in the human group; group activities, play, decision-making, planning, goal-setting, conflict resolution are all purposeful programs to these ends.

The resolution of each crisis or task and the strengthening of ego function while progressing through the developmental stages are particularly effective means of preventing breakdown at a later date. The support of peers, the provision of emotional nutrients, the experiences of closeness and trust, the exercise of self-determination and its concomitant, self-respect, are also the most effective kinds of deterrents to dysfunction known today. These seem to me to be the functions of a great many group services agencies. One has to be simpleminded to suggest that it is better to wait until people become ill to render services of a curative nature rather than seek by all means available to provide preventive innoculations and, even more so, to assign low status to the health builders.

Group services agencies grew out of communion, companionship, and community self-help. Since their inception, they have been rooted in the most democratic of traditions. For example, settlement workers lived in the community and were neighbors, the YWCA built its organization on local committees, the scouting movement depends upon volunteers for its operation. Social groupwork has always had a commitment to helping people live in a democracy and to citizenship education. Until most recently, every responsible writer affirmed the democratic essential of groupwork. Freedom of decision and choice with responsibility have been the spirit of social work endeavor and the heart of social groupwork. These seem to me to be the stated commitments of group services agencies.

The great names in social work have been associated with social change. Well-baby clinics, free milk, provision of medical services, birth control, housing, workmen's compensation, protection of women, civil rights, and many more have been pioneered through the Henry Street Settlement, Chicago Commons, Recreation Rooms and Settlement, Toynbee Hall, Hudson Guild, Grand Street Settlement, the YWCA, church agencies, the CYO, Jewish community centers, and many others. Social action has been an inherent and inextricable part of social groupwork throughout its history. Neighborhood development, community organization, and programs for social change evolved in group services agencies long before the present advocates in community organization ever dreamed of them. Advocacy itself was a settlement concept in practice.

The model presented in this book operates on a matching conceptualization and holds that the environment as well as the individual must adjust in order to provide maximization for one and all. I have cited these as propositions in social work through group process. They seem to me to be the supporting frameworks of the group services organizations.

I believe it was Fritz Redl and his associates who developed the "life space interview" idea. Many writers in the group treatment field speak of the group as a "slice of life." The idea that the group experience is a here-and-now microcosm, and as such is a medium for testing, practicing, becoming aware, and learning new behaviors goes back into the early history of groupwork in the agencies. The belief that the worker is a model, that he does not dominate, and that he is an enabler of the group process is part of the fabric of groupwork and it seems to me that these concepts have been the woof and the warp of group services agencies.

How has it happened that the group services agencies and social groupwork as it is written and taught have become estranged? Some of the reasons are that there is an obvious failure of communication as well as a possible loss of respect and diminution of trust. There has been some anxiety on the part of the agencies regarding the threat of domination by theorists and super-scientists. There may be some lessening of a commitment to human beings. Nevertheless, social work through group process is not only applicable to the traditional group services agency but it is a sine qua non. It is not the only method; multi-service agencies can use a wide variety of methods, but I believe that social work through group process is an essential modality.

Social work through group process is method. I have been presenting one proposed model. A method is a way of accomplishing specified goals, but one must be wary of goals being so specific that they enforce rigidity and by so doing create a domination of their own. Specific goals are bounded by one's knowledge and vision and allow little leeway for those things of which we have never dared to dream. The human spirit is boundless and, as such, should not be fettered to the limit of perception.

A method does not prescribe objectives nor does it determine policy. This point has been missed by many boards of directors and agency administrations. Social groupwork does not tell the agency what its purposes ought to be, how it must be structured, or what to do. Social groupwork is

165

a "way" and if it can accomplish the agency's purposes it can be used. As a method, it can be applied, modified, and fitted. It is about these applications that now I want to write.

For some time, group services agencies were criticized by social workers because the groups therein were led by volunteers, part-time workers, and "untrained" workers. They were accused of being unprofessional (a very awful thing to be to say the least). They were asked, "How can you possibly be doing social work with groups when your groups are not being led by social workers with MSW's? To do social work, the groups must be led by graduates. You do not belong in social work." They were accused of using the professionals inappropriately by assigning them to supervisory jobs, middle management, and administration.

Then one day, first out of pressure, then out of necessity, and finally out of rationalization, social workers devised terms for untrained workers like paraprofessional, indigenous, and subprofessional, and announced that agencies not using these people were not being professional. Testimonials were written to attest that paraprofessionals were more effective than MSW's; they were able to communicate better; clients trusted them; they had empathy; they understood the culture; and so on.

There followed a flutter of excitement about training subprofessionals, supervising subprofessionals, and recruiting them. Let it be known that there is a rich literature in groupwork on these subjects but, unfortunately, it is being ignored by many in their "newly found" discoveries. These areas were pioneered by Sidney Lindenberg, Margaret Williamson, Sorrenson and Dimock, and researched by people like Daniel Thurz. Volunteers and part-time workers were used to lead groups, and to counsel groups in agencies and cabin groups in camps.

I am relating this history because I want to affirm to the group services agencies that they can and always could utilize social work through group process with paraprofessional group leaders. Where groups present special problems or require more skilled social work, it would be common sense to use better trained and more experienced workers.

166

The proper utilization of manpower is an administrative question. A mutual-aid model makes use of
differing levels of worker competences. There will
be more B.A. social work graduates and more paraprofessionals in the social work job force in the
future. The appropriate utilization of these people
in casework and community development will have
to be more carefully thought out than has been done
up to now.

In the group services agencies, the MSW personnel are best utilized when, in addition to con-
ducting especially needy groups, they train, act
as consultants to group leaders, and help in formu-
lating diagnoses and helping approaches. This connotes colleague consultation and not supervision.
I would urge the group services agencies to convert
to "group supervision" and to conduct the training
and development of group leaders through the model
described in this book.

It would be unjustified to leave the reader
with the impression that the agencies have been
paragons of virtue in their use of paraprofessionals as group leaders; they have not. They have
not selected carefully nor with discrimination so
as, for example, to weed out the dominators; they
have done poorly with orientation and the induction of workers into the culture of social work;
they have been guilty of malfeasance in training
and also in not providing effective consultation.
Some have done better than others but few have
done well. However, the misuse of such personnel
is no argument against the validity of their proper use. Group services agencies can do social
work through group process with group leaders who
do not have masters' degrees.

Most group services agencies and multi-func-
tional agencies have specific points of view to
which they are committed. Their functions include
important objectives, ideologies, and missions.
Each agency has its tradition, philosophy, and
specialized purpose. These purposes include such
things as fostering Jewish identification, promoting Christian brotherhood and sisterhood, character development, promoting Americanism, and the
like. The fact that an agency has a purpose, such
as these examples, does not preclude the use of
social groupwork nor does it prevent the utiliza-

167

tion of the model presented in this book.

The agency is part of the impinging environment of the member and the group and its philosophical orientation is a fact of life, that is, reality. The agency and the members can be engaged meaningfully in a process whereby they seek a matching which will facilitate communication and allow for transaction with each other toward mutually acceptable goals for the ultimate benefit of both.

People become members of group services agencies voluntarily. When they do so, the agency apprises them of its purpose. Many people join because of the function of the agency. The act of joining is the first step in the formation of a mutual agreement and it is the obligation of the agency to present its purpose clearly, honestly, and openly so that a contract can eventuate in good faith. The details of that contract and the relationship are worked out over a period of time starting with an intake process.

If the agency does not state its purpose, or if it states it obliquely or only hints at it, it is misrepresenting itself and is manipulating by imposing on the members. Such practices are more like the morals of the marketplace and have no place in a social agency. The clarity of the purposes makes it possible for the parties to negotiate and to transact. If the agency has something worthwhile and useful to offer, it need not conceal its objectives. However, if it is uncertain about its usefulness and validity, its objectives will not be accomplished, even if it "sugar coats" its position.

The agency has every right to present its point of view and to demonstrate its rationale. The member retains the right to accept or reject it, use it, or let it be. The goals of the members are not subverted merely because the agency believes as it does, as long as it shares these beliefs openly.

There are important practical points which must be stressed. The agency must act and behave in accordance with its beliefs. If only agency staff members would realize that they would be infinitely more successful by living and demonstrating their ideologies and purposes than by imposing them, lecturing, proselytizing, and manipulating. Were they to behave in accordance with their stated beliefs, the transaction of the member to the agency environment would eventuate in favorable outcomes.

It is not my purpose or my prerogative to elaborate on this observation but to point out that if agencies and staff do not demonstrate democracy in action, love of one's fellowman, the teachings of Jesus Christ, or Jewish values and beliefs, then these purposes, no matter how often stated or how lofty, will not be achieved.

Rituals and tribal dances, role playing, art shows, music week, and song fests that lack sincerity and are devoid of human spirit are not the essence of identification and cultural survival. The noise is so loud that the message the agencies say they wish to send often cannot be heard. If agencies exploit their workers without mercy they cannot promote brotherly love. If agencies deny democratic process in their administration and defend indefensible societal sins, they cannot talk people into "the American Way." For agencies that can show the way and confront their members directly without subterfuge in the encounter, the propositions of groupwork in this matching model are appropriate.

When the agency shows the way and is frank, the concerns of the members about any contradictions between it and the members can be discussed. The assumptions can be explicated, examined, and challenged. The rights of each can be protected and both can change and grow through the process of mutuality. The most promising aspects of these changes lie in whether the agency is significant in the lives of the members. All of the structure, lofty purpose, and theory are to no avail unless the members regard the group and the agency as significant and believe that it can be trusted. The agency is significant if it meets the needs of the members and is infused with ego recognition, closeness, and freedom. Reinforcement is based upon reward.

These concepts are so devastatingly simple

that they leave one feeling that there must be more
to it. They are so sentimental sounding that they
are derisively called idealistic. They are so difficult to achieve that workers instead of working
with them look for panaceas, gadgets, gimmicks, and
techniques. Workers should stop struggling to find
techniques and fads and live by what they profess.

I have argued that the worker must be himself
and meet the members as a person. I present that
idea now in larger terms, that is, the agency must
be itself and what it purports to be, meeting the
members and the group with honesty equal to that
required of the worker. There is no contradiction
between this point of view and social work through
group process. The agency can have its beliefs and
purposes, and if it is straightforward it will have
no need to control, superimpose, hide, or push.
Its stance will help the members find themselves
and move in the direction of adaptation and matching with the agency, to the benefit of the agency
and its goals and the members and their goals, as
long as the members are free to arrive at their
own conclusions and make their own decisions.

There are practice problems involved. The
members may perceive the purposes of the agency as
being quite different from what they actually are.
A typical example occurs when the members regard
the agency as a recreation center and not as a
social agency. This happens not only because the
members want it so but because there is ambivalence,
conflict, and lack of resolution about agency purpose on the part of the board and the staff and,
consequently, the noise prevails. It occurs because group leaders are not committed to the stated
purposes of the agency. It happens because those
leaders came through the agency program as members
and were not confronted with its beliefs, assumptions, and consequences and, therefore, did not
resolve in their own minds the relation of the
purpose of the agency to their own goals.

Assuming that the members do regard the agency purpose incorrectly, as recreation in this instance, then what?

1. The basic needs of the members must still
be met. One assumes that they do want closeness
and interpersonal validation but have been condi-

tioned not to expect these in a social agency and to fear and not to trust. The fact that they seek recreation does not rule out their other needs; in fact, it may be their way of seeking to meet them.

2. Recreation is a medium and not an end. It is a vehicle through which other needs can be met. The relation between recreation and needs has been spelled out by Slavson and others.[1]

3. One begins where the members are by providing them with the vehicle. Through it the worker negotiates a contract by presenting the agency purpose to the members and helping them to see that there is no disagreement between them as he proposes to help them reach their own goals. Interests and goals are not synonymous.

4. The recreation program in a group services agency provides the medium through which the agency demonstrates and enables interpersonal need-meeting, ego-strengthening, self-realization, closeness, freedom from control, and the like. It is less what they do and more how it is done that counts. The program provides a demonstration of agency purpose and beliefs, a means to purposes, an emphasis on meeting needs, and a confrontation with the worker.

5. The members are free to leave if they do not want what the agency has to offer.

6. In groupwork, one starts where the members are but, hopefully, does not settle for leaving them there, not growing, changing, and moving toward their goals.

The formulation then is: believe, act in accordance with those beliefs and share them with the members honestly in the formulation of a contract.

The points being made, although they are specific to the group services agency, apply also to other social agencies; for example, in a hospital where the patients perceive the group as "head shrinking," or the institution where the children

---

[1]S. R. Slavson, <u>Recreation and the Total Personality</u> (New York: Association Press, 1946).

see the group as representing adult authority and
develop a culture to neutralize it.

A second practice problem involves values.
Values were discussed briefly in another subsection
and I said we would return to the subject. Many
people who are prominent in the development of
social groupwork established the premise that
groupwork transmits social values and that this is
an important aspect of practice.[1]

The times in which we live are in a state of
rapid change. Men have just landed on the moon,
while it was but sixty years ago that Orville
Wright set a record for sustained flight by re-
maining aloft for a few hours. Social values are
culturally determined and arise out of the imperatives of the times. They come into being to fulfill the needs of man and are related to the social
thought of the period in which they develop. When
changes in the world and in man's situation occurred
much more slowly than they do today, there was an
opportunity for values to keep pace with our way
of life. When changes took many years to evolve
and society was relatively stable, social values
also remained constant over long periods of time.

Today, change is cataclysmic. Scientific progress, technology, and communication have expanded
the horizons so that social values which were suited
to rural cultures, frontier cultures, horse-and-
buggy living, and the like are no longer applicable.
Pierre Berton, for example, speaks of yesterday's
values as myths that have no validity in a post-
Puritan age.[2] He refers to values such as "Idle
hours breed mischief," "Work hard to get ahead,"
"Handouts kill initiative," and the like. These
are values which may have been pertinent in a
Puritan America but now plot to inhibit freedom
from useless toil, freedom from want, freedom from
exploitation. They are not germane today and must
be reassessed in the same way that we have re-

---

[1]Saul Bernstein, Grace Coyle, Clara Kaiser,
Gisela Konopka, Dorothea Spellman, and Dorothea
Sullivan, to mention a few.

[2]Pierre Berton, The Smug Minority (New York:
J. B. Lippincott Co., 1968).

evaluated colonialism, imperialism, slavery, and war which were considered honorable at one time.

Some values we believe are enduring and universal in Western civilization. These we believe are good in and of themselves because they support human enhancement. Other values are more transitory and temporary and are not central to man's self-realization. For example, long hair, dress, language, music, dancing, art forms, sexual behavior, and the like are temporal and superficial when compared with the dignity of man, love, freedom, prohibition of exploitation, honesty in human relations, intimacy, and the like. These values which are "bonum per se" are good because they are pertinent to man's condition of living together with other people and achieving maximization.

Values are not viable unless they are one's own, and they are inhibiting if they are not relevant to man's being and becoming. If a social value is relevant, meaningful, and makes sense, the members can and will arrive at it through an examination of it, of the basic assumptions that underlie it, and by comparing their own goals with the consequences of acting upon the values they already hold or proposed new ones. In any other way, values are symbols of external control. In the agency they can be tested, explored, and accepted if the agency program demonstrates and supports them. The way to have values established and internalized is not for the agency to struggle to transmit values. Values that are apposite are developed through experiences; by programs which make them explicit, validate them, and reinforce them by example; by testing their assumptions; and by finding them useful. Such values as are developed in this way should also be reinforced throughout the total program as well as throughout the entire agency operation.

The principle here is that we do not transmit values but we enable the members to find their own. We do voice our own values and our reasoning behind them, we do promulgate the values of the profession and the agency for scrutiny and challenge. We also will challenge and confront the members. We do not transmit, impose, exhort; but as partners we will seek together for the social values that have meaning for the members in a modern world.

This process does not require sitting around a table in intellectual talk sessions. It can take place on the gym floor, on a sightseeing trip, in the ward, in a waiting room, or on the floor in front of a fire on a camping weekend. Social work through group process is an appropriate method for the social agency that has an ideology or special purpose to use.

A third practice problem concerns organizational structure. A club program is not a requisite for social work through group process. Groupwork is a method for helping people and as a method it can be used in many settings, formal and informal. It is not necessary to have structured, small groups. While it is true that some kinds of organization make successful outcomes more probable, they are not prerequisite to the use of the method.

It is reasonable to suggest that the method is most usable with small groups having stable compositions, where the grouping has been made in relation to the purpose, and where the duration is long enough for intimacy to evolve. These are the ideal conditions for which we strive. When conditions are not ideal, results will not be as great, will take longer to achieve, and will require more skilled personnel.

However, the propositions set forth in this model can be applied in a lounge program, with a pickup group, in the gym, with a team, or on a hike. They apply in a ward, in a cottage, in a residence, in a physical rehabilitation meeting room, or in the visitors' lounge in a hospital.

The model presented here does not rely on structure and, therefore, the group need not be set up as a "group." In a rehabilitation center, or a veterans' hospital, for example, one might not set up a formal group program. A group worker on the staff might not be used to meet with scheduled and organized groups but rather to work with groupings when and where they happen. It is not valid then for agencies not to use social work through group process because they have no clubs or formal groups. Give them people, a worker, and a stance, and they are in business.

CHAPTER 8

NOTES ON GROUP THERAPY AND
FAMILY GROUP COUNSELING

Group Therapy

Therapy is a process that liberates individuals from inhibiting fears in a good and reliable relationship, frees the ego potential for creative self-realization, and facilitates the birth of a real self. Group therapy is that process of liberation through the group process.

The purposes of group therapy include the improvement of reality-testing, the aiding of socialization, the fostering of psychological aptitudes, and the provision of motivation for continued change. These purposes are accomplished through new identifications, mutual support, diminished feelings of isolation, release of impounded anger, improved self-esteem, and improved self-assertion.

A major conception in modern approaches to group therapy is that the reactions and feelings in the therapy group are similar to those that the members experience outside of the group and, hence, what is learned in the group is to be used by them to guide their behavior elsewhere. It is an important theme in this book that anxiety can be both a result of and a defense and protection against closeness in interpersonal relations. The greater the closeness in the treatment group in the early stages, the more anxiety will be expressed. This results in group disorganization, acting-out, hostility, silences, tardiness, absences, scapegoating, and competitiveness. The release of impounded feelings and the opportunity for self-assertion in an atmosphere which invites trust by guaranteeing freedom raises self-esteem and diminishes withdrawal and depression. The methods through which help is given include practical support, emotional support, and educational reorientation of the coping mechanisms of the group members through learning experiences.

The key to group therapy is in the experience rather than in insight. A democratic experience is an essential and the current happenings in the

group situation are the content of the treatment.
The here-and-now is the group process, the group
members are the therapists, and the medium is mutual support and help.

Group therapy as we know it professionally is
a relatively recent development. One of the first
known practitioners of group therapy in this country was Dr. Joseph Pratt.[1] In Boston, Dr. Pratt
treated tuberculosis patients as a group. His
treatment focus was to have the patients discuss
their feelings and attitudes which affected the
management of their illness, and he offered them
advice and reassurance. Jane Addams, as a social
worker, met with groups of narcotic addicts around
their addiction problem. On a recent extended
tour of the Orient, I found that group treatment
of drug addiction has been the only method which
has achieved any degree of success there.

Groups were not used much in social work in
the early days and Mary Richman advised social
workers to turn their attention to the use of
groups in the early twenties. Social groupwork
began about 1925 in this country.

People knew about the therapeutic values of
the group long before the nineteen hundreds. Med-
icine men in primitive tribes have used group involvement and ritual to cure the ill and to influence the spirit for centuries. When Christianity
was young and, even before that, when the Jews were
wandering tribes, religious leaders used group
methods to exorcise torturing spirits from people
who were thought to be possessed. Many religious
ceremonies and folk traditions are reminiscent of
group treatment, and many religious rituals today
deal specifically with problems of behavior and
thought which we would label as mental or emotional illness.

Indians in Guatemala, Ecuador, and the Yucatan
engage in what is very much like a diagnostic-
study interrogation, a cathartic confession; a
group cure led by a professional healer. It is

---

[1]Max Rosenbaum and Milton Berger, eds., Group
Psychotherapy and Group Function (New York: Basic
Books, Inc., 1968), pp. 3-22.

believed that this custom has been handed down from the ancient Mayans.

Aside from religious practices, changes in behavior or social functioning occur through joining a social, political, or communal movement such as an anti-war organization, the Communist Party, or the Shakers. One is socialized into new and appropriate behavior through the media of commitment to group goals; the expectation and receipt of social rewards, contagion, identification, sanctions, and group pressure. It seems that people seek and are sought by groups that offer solutions to their problems of living. When one becomes a member one accepts the tenets, norms, values, beliefs, and prescriptions for behavior of the group.

The normal processes of change which take place through group membership and process have been adapted and consciously used by professional healers. An example of this can be seen in the structuring of the milieu in therapy.

As group therapy has evolved, many different schools of thought have arisen with their own unique brand of practice. However, there are several discernible trends in the field today. Treatment methods do not come into being in isolation. There is a close relationship among social thought, the belief system, the cultural core (economic, militaristic, religious, humanistic, and so forth), and how people live and treat each other, the goals they have, and what they prize.

These characteristics of a people are reflected in what they believe illness to be (possessed by spirits, hexed, invaded by virus, chemical or electrical disturbance, learned roles, and emotional disturbance) and how they devise treatment. Treatment modalities in the social-helping professions tend to change and adapt to the social trends and social thought of the times. It is not happenstance that, recently, group methods have become so popular in social work, psychiatry, and psychology. Groupwork is fast becoming a preferred strategy and a treatment of choice. As we have seen, the group approach tends to flatten out the differences between man and man, between professional and patient, as well as attesting to the power of peers. This trend is reflected in our culture as one sees the increasing pressure and demands for equality.

The theory base and practice in group therapy today narrow the gap between practitioner and client, between life situations and treatment situations, and there is an attempt to practice democracy in therapy. Of course, this is not universally true and much practice is autocratic, but theory and practice are being liberalized. Group therapy flourishes in America and England but it never grew on the Continent because much of Europe has been dominated by non-democratic, political systems. This is basic to an understanding of the assumptions, the practice theory, and the methodology of group treatment currently.

Group treatment has a potential for putting powerful forces into the hands of group members. It supports self-determining qualities. It is a form in which authority comes from the most democratic of processes and in which pressure for change is offered by peers rather than coming from an authoritarian source. Democracy is the hallmark of group treatment and it rests upon a belief in egalitarianism. The group equalizes the availability of treatment and resources.

There are several current trends. Some of these are that the group is a current reality, that it is a slice of life, and that the group is egalitarian. Therapy is provided by the group members who participate as peers in a democratic, therapeutic community. In addition, there is a growing acceptance of the interrelationship, interdependence, and interpenetration of the person both physically and psychically, the social situation, and the culture. Any modification of the group and of the individual members is interdependent. It is no longer profitable to speak of the social, the psychological, or the biological as if we had hold of three separate problems, three different fields, and three levels of logical analysis.

Still another trend is seen in the acceptance of an existential stance. Some of the ideas that influence the increasing interest in group treatment were discussed previously. They are that one cannot predict the precise consequences of therapeutic interventions and, hence, the group process is more important than the therapist; the group is the here-and-now experience and as such is life, reality, and is significant; and that the essence of treatment is to enable the member to be free.

Social workers with the exception of social groupworkers, however, have tended to work with groups as though the worker was the therapeutic component performing before an audience. Such incongruous terms as group casework or casework with a group have emerged. These reflect confused thinking. There remains a temptation to use the authority of the position of the worker instead of allowing the group to be the therapeutic medium and, therefore, freeing the group to treat its members.

Papanek suggests that a democratic group must have free and full communication.[1] If one wishes members to move toward self-determination and to relinquish maladaptive solutions to problems, the worker must facilitate freedom of communication among the members and encourage democratic functioning. This implies that the members are not tools but are the prime movers in mutual help. Moreover, the group experience is the here-and-now; it is the experience, and as such it is the arena for learning adaptive social functioning. These concepts are very different from those wherein the primary emphasis is on insight, resolution of historical intrapsychic conflicts, genetic reconstruction, or dealing with transference phenomena with the therapist.

Many workers who were trained in a one-to-one methodology do not believe that the group can be the therapeutic medium; they do not trust the group or the group process and they do not subscribe to the idea that treatment lies in the current group-living experiences. The worker is not a change agent--a term in popular usage today in some circles. He is not an intervener, an expert, or a master in the control of therapeutic processes. He may like to think that he is or he may need to

[1]Helen Papanek, "Psychotherapy without Insight: Group Therapy as Milieu Therapy," _Journal of Individual Psychology_, Vol. XVII, No. 2 (November, 1961), 187.

think so. The skill of the group therapist is in facilitating or freeing the group member to be and to become.

Family Group Counseling

In sharp contrast to the democratic stance which is being promoted in group therapy, family therapy and family group therapy seem to be consciously worker dominated. For example, Virginia Satir says that all family therapists, no matter how differently they devise their interventions, soon come to the realization that if they are going to be successful change agents they cannot continue to be passive.[1]

The major modes in family group treatment are either treating individuals within a family group interview or manipulating the family group in order to change the behavior of individual members. In the first instance, the tool is the worker who practices individual therapy to change an individual member within a group setting. In the second instance, the worker remains primarily the therapeutic agent and he alters the family system to influence the behavior of the individual members. The members are not seen as helping agents in the way in which one conceptualizes group therapy in either instance. It is the premise in this book that a social worker who is functioning as a family group therapist should perform as a social worker, which should mean that the family should solve its own problems, albeit with help, and as a group therapist, which should mean through group process. It is puzzling that the family treatment models in vogue in social work show little awareness of the group process or of group dynamics. They show almost no application of group theory although they have the word "group" in the title.

In a variety of models we can divide the family therapists who have written about their work as dominators or interacters, but not as enablers. The dominators are vigorous personalities who are able to hold their audiences spellbound. They have a clear and explicit sense of their own values and their own goals which they hope, in one way or

---

[1]Satir, _Conjoint Family Therapy_, p. 112.

another, to get the family in treatment to adopt. The interacters tend to have less compelling public personalities and are less imposing. They present themselves to families as themselves and as therapists, but they also have a repetoire of other roles which they can assume when they think this is indicated to help family members act differently from the way they have in the past.

In my opinion, Ackerman[1] and Satir are dominators. Dr. Ackerman is a physician and a psychiatrist; Satir is a psychiatric social worker. Both generally make more statements in a session than any family member. Although they allege that their aim is to promote interaction between the family members, they seem to attempt to do this by establishing star-shaped communication with themselves at the center. In fairness to Dr. Ackerman, he is very knowledgeable about group structure and dynamics.

He attacks the family interaction by watching it for verbalizations, gestures, and interactional clues to the more primitive relations of sex, aggression, and helpless dependency in the family. He then tickles the defenses (denial, hypocrisy, and projection) against these, forcing members to be more open with him and with each other. He also lends the family his pleasures in life, jokes, good sex, and limited aggression.

Satir presents herself to the family as a teacher and an expert in communication. She says that the therapist must show his patients that he is going somewhere and that he knows where he is going. She believes that the patients come to him because he is an expert and he must accept himself as such.[2]

There are other therapists who can be classified as dominators and who, even though they see the family together, do not seem to work through group process.[3] Some writers allege that they

---

[1]Nathan Ackerman, Treating the Troubled Family (New York: Basic Books, Inc., 1966).

[2]Satir, Conjoint Family Therapy, p. 160.

[3]Examples are: Murray Bowen, Salvatore Minuchin, and Ronald Tharp.

have regard for the internal power of a family to solve its own problems but they reveal that they manipulate covertly to effect changes on their own terms.[1] Leading interacters are Carl Whitaker, Alfred Friedman, Ivan Boszormenyi, James Framo, and Normal Paul. They are not dominators but their terminology leads me to conclude that their methodology is similar to that of traditional psychoanalytical therapy.

These models, that is, dominators, interacters, psychoanalytical therapists, and also advocates for the use of co-therapists are inappropriate to social work. In contrast, Andrew Ferber and C. C. Beels[2] believe in systems analysis, communication theory, and role theory. They postulate that the purpose of family therapy is to change the relationships in the family system. In this model, the members' self-centered preoccupations, past and present, shift to a concern with present and future interactions in the family group. The family system is the pattern of relationships between members of the family or the actions of the family members which have systems properties of responsive interdependence.

To view the family as a system creates difficulties for most practicing family therapists, or at least those who publish. Most models in the literature present the worker as the one who influences the family relationships. They speak of being scientifically objective in regard to behavior, but somehow in the diagnosis, some member is blamed for the disturbances. In a systems analysis, no one can be to blame for a system dysfunction because everyone is part of the action and each cause is both a cause and an effect. Ferber and Beels see the family as a system, and the interaction as the family program. Social workers are in the habit of perceiving the people in family treatment but not seeing the program. The family has a script, as in a drama, and the members re-

---

[1]Gerald Zuk, Jay Haley, Don Jackson, etc.

[2]Andrew S. Ferber and C. C. Beels, "Changing Family Behavior Programs," in Family Therapy, Ackerman, ed. (New York: Little, Brown & Co., 1969).

hearse it and replay it repeatedly. Ferber and
Beels make the family members aware of this stage
play--the actor's gesture, the up-staging and
blocking, the "business"--and they help them to
rewrite or restage the play.

Most social workers would view the family as
interaction between people as in a tennis match.
A group therapist would see it as a figured and
synchronous dance pattern such as a ballet or a
folk dance.

Generally speaking, social work writers fall
short of the concept of group treatment when discussing family group treatment. Sanford N. Sherman
talks about influencing the egos of each family
member and the adaptations between family members.[1]
The title of his article speaks of sociology but
his writings show little evidence of group process.
Like Frances L. Beatman, Celia Mitchell, John Bell,
and others he practices individual casework in a
group. Arthur L. Leader suggests that workers assume an active, authoritative role in family group
treatment.[2]

Frances H. Shurz believes in family treatment,
she says, and she advocates it when family problems
are interpersonal, relational, and involve adolescents. She says that family treatment facilitates
changes in modes of communication and in role behavior. The fact that she is writing about adolescence and identifies group concepts might lead one
to assume that there would be reason to practice
family treatment in the context of group treatment.[3]

However, Mrs. Shurz was asked at an institute
in Pittsburgh whether she thought her workers needed

---

[1]Sanford N. Sherman, "The Sociological Character of Family Group Treatment," Social Casework
(April, 1964), 195-201.

[2]Arthur L. Leader, "Role of Intervention in
Family Group Treatment," Social Casework (June,
1964), 327-32.

[3]Frances H. Shurz, "The Crisis of Adolescence
in Family Life," Social Casework (April, 1967),
209-15.

some understanding of the group process and group dynamics to do family treatment. She replied that she did not and went on to say that her staff had no such training and did not need it to practice. The basis of treatment she said was in understanding intra- and interpsychic dynamics and for the worker to know when and how to intervene.

It is my observation that most social workers who work with families as groups actually block the group from finding its own way, stop group interaction, and resist the group process. The worker, who becomes central or who takes over, usurps the roles which belong to the family members. The skill of the worker should lie in freeing the group members, by enabling the group, by showing how, but not by being the star actor or doer.

There is great promise in family group therapy through group process. The propositions set forth in this book apply to family group therapy. It is to be hoped that more social workers will begin to apply the principles of group therapy to family treatment and also that more groupworkers will get into a practice that up to now has been dominated by analytically-oriented caseworkers, psychiatrists, and psychologists. Instead of following these traditional approaches in a family group, social work could develop a most dynamic family-group-treatment model in the manner of social work through group process.

In such an approach, the family will set its own goals and make its own decisions. The family therapist will help the family to find its strengths and seek its own ways of reaching its goals. Once goals are clarified, the family can begin to work on its task. The worker listens to see if the members are indeed working. If they are evading, he will point it out and challenge them. His faith in their capacity to provide mutual aid, if the members can be free to collaborate, focuses his efforts on helping them to discover and deal with those forces which obstruct their work.

Family therapy as discussed here does not rest upon the usual conceptions of pathology or illness. This model rests upon the idea that deviating behavior is a solution to a problem and, more often than not, that which appears to be dysfunctional or malappropriate may be a means of surviving in an otherwise intolerable interpersonal relationship. It is being suggested that many such dysfunctions have their inception in patterns categorized by domination-submission, which give rise to a fear of intimacy, as well as in repetitious family games. Much family therapy as described in the literature duplicates these patterns of autocracy, dominance, and gamesmanship by the therapist. One can apply to family group therapy the same concepts that have pervaded this book; namely, equality, self-determination, and mutual aid.

To paraphrase Lao Tze, a family group therapist is one who works with a family and when he is done the members say, "Behold what we have accomplished by ourselves."

CHAPTER 9

CRITIQUE OF SMALL GROUP THEORY

In Section I, I gave an overview of designs currently being used in social work primarily in working with groups. I did not include those which suggest that groupwork should rely heavily on small group theory. There is a movement of this kind; some schools teach groupwork from what they are pleased to call an empirical base, by which they mean small group research. At least one eminent educator is engaged in writing a book about social groupwork which is based on small group theory. One cannot ignore these writers or teachers and, consequently, I have chosen to discuss the pros and cons in a separate chapter.

Many of the so-called new insights about groups which are credited to small group research are not new at all. Much of this information about groups was common knowledge among social group-workers when I began to lead groups thirty years ago. Their conscious awareness of group properties, factors, and dynamics was gained through direct practice and involvement with groups of various kinds over long periods of time. Such knowledge is indeed empirical.

It is argued that this kind of experience is suspect and that it must be subjected to rigorous scientific testing, and I agree. However, much of the research on small groups reported in books and journals is not applicable to social work practice. Some of the reasons are that the studies are usually not conducted with genuine psyche or peer groups; most studies are not related to the personal or growth needs of the people in the groups; there is no differentiation made between and among different kinds of groups and purposes; the intent is to learn how to use the group for ulterior motives which is not consonant with social work objectives; the research, by and large, describes or pictures what happens in groups but it does not explain how it happens, nor does it address itself to what one can do to help groups improve group functioning in keeping with social work objectives; and the research has been done on groups without social

workers while the essence of social work is the
social work process with a social worker.

In order to develop a design for social work
practice or theory, one must establish at least
four components. These are: the cause of the problem, the method of action, the probable outcomes,
and the evidence that the problem has been solved
or partially solved and that the action effected
the outcome. Small group theory has helped us to
understand many of the causes of group dysfunction
and, also, of individual behavior in groups. However, there is little or no evidence that it has
been much help in defining methods of action, or
in developing relationships between outcomes and
action by a social worker or by social work methods, or in providing the means for assessing such
results, if any.

Also, the weaknesses that I am identifying
are due partially to the failure of social workers to conduct the necessary research. Be that
as it may, as of this moment small group theory
does not provide a basis for social work through
group process.

There are practice designs, based upon small
group theory and research, that do relate methods
of action to probable outcomes, but these are designs that manipulate social variables in order to
produce change in people's behavior. Manipulation
of this kind is not appropriate in social work; it
does not foster growth or ego strength and it is
too easily subverted to ends that are chosen by
others for reasons that are not always in the best
interest of the group member.

I am not criticizing small group theory or the
research per se. They are important, and the insights gained are valuable in the pursuit of knowledge about groups. Much of these findings are ex-
tremely valuable to the social worker. They form
the basis of my schema for diagnosing group functioning. Currently, this material is of inestima-
ble value in sociology, social psychology, and organizational theory but it is not the kind of base
I would recommend for a social-work-through-group-
process theory or for practice.

Small group theory is of value to us because

it tells us about how people act in groups under certain circumstances and how certain groups behave. We are aware that groups have the power to pressure members to conform and that members tend to accept the group culture and the norms that are central to the group's existence. When in a group, one tends not to express opinions which are contrary to group opinion. Group members tend to conform to group values because they view such conformity as maximizing their chances for achieving individual goals.

We know that groups can apply sanctions to members and punish them. A group can deny access to its resources and rejection is one of the consequences of deviation in highly cohesive groups. This as well as other factors greatly influence self-image. When an individual is in a social situation he tends to react toward himself in the same way that he thinks others would react toward him. One tends to accept information obtained from others in this manner as valid.

We know a great deal about power and power hierarchy in groups; we have learned that status and position are related to power. We are aware that persons in positions of power are reluctant to share or relinquish power, and that power gives people great advantages in the accession of information and need-meeting resources. Those who lack power also lack communication and the resources that would enhance their self-image or meet basic human needs.

We know that all groups develop subgroups and that these reflect sociometric patterns of acceptance and rejection. Social distance is a function of these patterns and it can force the weakest of the group even farther from the resources.

Small group theory helps us to know how positions and structure solidify, how roles become patterned, how people are held in habitual expectations and performances, and how such group prescriptions can perpetuate behaviors. The corollary is that when the group structure or patterns change, individuals are influenced to change also. Moreover, we know that the dynamics of most groups do not foster or encourage creativity in the members.

These foregoing factors and others tell us a good deal about decision-making. We find that group decisions are influenced greatly by status, position, conformity, and by sequences of communication or information. We also know that leadership can and does manipulate the factors in order to influence the decisions and also that the minority subgroup or member can have little effect on decisions in many kinds of groups.

To a great extent, small group research shows us that there is a fallacy in thinking that small groups function democratically. Social groupwork has been fooling itself in thinking that most small groups either train for democratic living, or that the isolates or minorities in them are helped through the usual group decision-making machinery.

Herbert J. Gans writes, "But while the American political structure often satisfies the majority, it also creates outvoted minorities who can be tyrannized and repressed by majority rule, such as the blacks, students, migrant workers, and many others. In the past, such minorities have had to rely on the goodwill of the majority, hoping that it would act morally, but it generally offered them only charity, if that much."[1] What he says about the larger political society is true also of groups. Many groups vote or make decisions with the same subgroup minorities habitually being outvoted or outinfluenced.

He goes on, "America has been a pluralistic society for almost a century, but the shortcomings of majority rule have not become a public issue before, mainly because previous generations of outvoted groups had other forms of redress?...Now this has changed...and more often than not, their demands are frustrated by the workings of majority rule.

"Thus, it becomes quite pertinent to ask whether majoritarian democracy is still viable, and whether the tradition of majority rule should not be re-examined."[3]

---

[1]Gans, "We Won't End the Urban Crisis until We End Majority Rule," p. 14.

[2]Ibid., p. 20.

[3]Ibid., p. 24.

The most needful member and the "client" in the social work group are comparable to the minority groups of which Gans speaks. They are the ones who get the leavings or who conform as the price they must pay for the tolerance of the more powerful members.

"I believe," Gans goes on, "that the time has come to modernize American democracy and adapt it to the needs of a pluralistic society, in short, to create a pluralistic democracy. A pluralistic form of democracy would not do away with majority rule, but would require systems of proposing and disposing which would take the needs of minorities into consideration, so that when majority rule has serious negative consequences, outvoted minorities would be able to achieve their most important demands, and not be forced to accept tokenism, or resort to despair or disruption."

In essence, Gans is suggesting a system wherein minorities can live and share more equitably in the country's resources and he would try to prevent minorities from being deprived and punished by a majority. He wants to prevent the tyrannization of minorities. My thesis relates this to the group and I want to prevent the tyrannization of those socially incompetent members who are in great need and who have been blocked in the past by their circumstances. It has been a theme in this book that people become ill, inadequate, or at least impoverished by depriving environments and I am arguing against setting up groups in social work which duplicate and perpetuate this oppression and deprivation.

Let us return to an examination of the critique of small group theory as a basis for social work with groups.

The studies are usually not conducted with genuine psyche or peer groups. Unless the members of a group have common interests, share a common fate and common norms for carrying out their functions, and have a stake in the outcomes of their group decisions, one cannot give much credence to research findings or generalize from them about real groups such as psyche groups. Groups which are formed in a laboratory and which deal with momentary pressures are not identical or even similar to regular ongoing groups. "A major factor conditioning the success of group discussion and group decision in changing group norms and individual behavior is the significance of the decisions for the people involved. One reason for the efficacy of the method is the involvement of people, the degree to which they can work out problems of importance to themselves and make decisions about their own fate....Discussion and decision about problems of importance invoke powerful individual forces of self-expression and self-determination."[1]

In addition to these questions of involvement or of group culture, there is also the fact that unless the group is a reference group to its members and meets their needs in some way, they are not really influenced by it so as to grow in it. Also, a group is not therapeutic in the group treatment sense until it reaches the stage of intimacy.[2] Small group research has not reported on these questions.

Most studies are not related to the personal or growth needs of the people in the group. Since groups in social work are for the primary purpose of enhancing social functioning and strengthening ego functioning, small-group-theory propositions are not wholly applicable. Most of the criteria used in the studies have to do with one or several of the following: task achievement, decision-making, behavioral change, attitudinal change, or production. One learns how to make groups more efficient but not necessarily how to help people to become more adequate. Learning theory is not included in this criticism because it has not been part of small-group theory.

There is no differentiation made between and among different kinds of groups and group purposes. This is a very serious defect in small group studies. The assumption is that all groups are alike and, therefore, one can just talk about groups and

---

[1]Katz and Kahn, The Social Psychology of Organizations, p. 401.

[2]Garland, Jones and Kolodny, "A Model for Stages of Development in Social Work Groups."

generalize from one group to any other. This is
not true. Helen Jennings differentiated nicely
between psyche and socio-groups, and there are
other classifications one could make. However,
for our purpose this suffices because some social
work theorists are making the error of indiscrim-
inately applying the findings about task groups
to psyche groups. Work groups in an industrial
plant, five students in a laboratory experiment,
a class committee, a council, a club, and a treatment group, are not identical. They may be alike
in many ways and there may be high-level abstrac-
tions which can be applied to all of them but, in
fact and in practice, they do differ. A main difference lies in purpose, and this is a vital distinction.

The intent is to learn how to use the group
for ulterior motives and this is not consonant
with social work objectives. Edwin J. Thomas has
done outstanding work in bringing together small-
group-research findings and developing theory.[1]
In examining his writings wherein he reports on
themes in small-group theory, one is struck by the
references to studies as, "to convert a group" or
"if one is seeking to convert members." Many experiments reported in the literature sought to
demonstrate how group method could be used to influence the individual as, for example, the problem of changing the informal norms of a work group
with respect to productivity (Bavelas), the use of
group discussion to gain acceptance for changes in
work methods in a garment factory (Coch and French),
to change food habits (Lewin), to effect rapid relearning to increase productivity, and to change
antagonism to cooperation (Coch and Franch).

Katz and Kahn seem to believe that the values
of group process in organizational settings can be
achieved only by seeking to simulate the true peer
groups. They point out that authority and status
figures inhibit group interaction because people are
less free to work through their own feelings and
ideas, and the resulting group decision may reflect
less of their own constructive solutions and produce less internalization. "A peer group does not

---

[1]Edwin J. Thomas, <u>Behavioral Science for
Social Workers</u> (New York: The Free Press, 1967).

lend itself readily to organizational structure in which the hierarchical principle is dominant. In fact, decision-making by peer groups could not be carried out fully without genuine modification of the hierarchical principle. The dynamic of the peer group is in contradiction to the hierarchical principle....A continuing problem in organizations is to produce a true peer-group situation in which members leave behind their other role investments and function only as citizens of the organization."[1]

Here one sees two points of view being expressed. On the one hand, the research theorists who seek to use the group as a tool in order to achieve organizational goals and, on the other, a plea to develop organizations wherein peer groups can function free from hierarchical influences. However, an industrial plant is not a social agency. When industry engages in small-group research, it endeavors to find ways of developing more productive employees, and this is fair. If it subscribes to the idea that involvement in decision-making by employees increases morale or commitment so that production rises, its interest is primarily in the individual in his work role. His enhancement is instrumental to the purposes of the industry. Such research projects do not fall within a social work frame of reference.

To date, small-group theory has described or pictured what happens in groups but it does not explain how it happens, nor does it address itself to what one can do to help groups improve social-functioning. This is a criticism which has been leveled at social science in general. It deals with an observation of what is. This is important and useful but since social work must do more than be able to see the problem, small-group theory is not yet a basis for group method.

The research has been done on groups without social workers while the essence of social work is the social work process with a social worker. The studies have told us what happens in a group when there is no social worker involved and when there is no social work being done. We can make predic-

---

[1]Katz and Kahn, _The Social Psychology of Organizations_, p. 405.

tions about what may happen in a group based upon an analysis of group factors and processes, but we receive no help from small-group theory about what happens to and in a group with a groupworker. We are not helped to know how the group process is affected by the worker's presence, his acts, or his stance. This leaves us with the premise that it is up to the social worker to apply the knowledge to practice and to fashion a method. Let us see what we can learn about this from Thomas who is foremost in the field of interpreters of small-group research.[1] The themes which are discussed below are selected from a voluminous literature which has been culled by Thomas.

Propinquity is a significant determinant of group membership. Thomas quotes Homans as saying that persons who interact frequently with one another tend to like one another. Of course this is not true as anyone knows who has worked in some interracial settlements and groups.

Newcomb is credited with psychological insights about interaction. When persons interact, the reward-punishment ratio is more often reinforcing than extinguishing and, on the whole, rewarding effects of interaction are more apt to be obtained from those with whom one interacts frequently. If interaction opportunities are equal, one will tend to like individuals who most resemble some other person whom one liked in the past. Interaction which is not rewarding would most likely result in dislike or affective neutrality whereas interaction that was reciprocally rewarding would be more apt to result in liking.

These comments lead to a discussion of attraction to a group and to group cohesiveness. One is attracted because one likes the people and because the group itself is an object of need. A second major source of attraction is the group as an instrument for satisfying needs outside the group. The more the group provides gratification of the needs of the members, the more likely they will remain in the group.

Groups high in cohesiveness appear to be more

---

[1]Thomas, <u>Behavioral Science for Social Workers</u>.

conducive to the security of the group members than those low in cohesiveness. Pressures toward uniformity vary directly with the cohesiveness of the group. There is resistance to disruption in a cohesive group. The level of performance is determined largely by group standards.

Individuals working together perform more vigorously on thought and motor activities though the quality of the work is not improved. Individuals make less extreme judgments when in a group than when alone. If the individual is actively impelled to take the role of another, he will more likely reflect the opinion of the other than if he can take this role passively.

In the final part of Thomas' review, he discusses power as researched by various authors.

I have summarized very briefly and sketchily some of the themes that Thomas selects from small-group theory and which he thinks are important for social work. The purpose is not to criticize Thomas, whose work is admired, nor to capitalize on his work by presenting these themes as important supports in this book. They are included because they illustrate that there is really little in small-group theory upon which to build a groupwork model even if one argues that it is up to the social worker to apply the knowledge.

Small-group theory has a far more important contribution to make to groupwork with groups, however. It teaches one that groups and group process operating without social work can be a devastating experience for many emotionally-deprived people and that the most important function of the worker is to help the group to face itself and its functioning.

Groups tend to develop structures, norms, and role patterns fairly early in their development. These properties fast become institutionalized so that they resist change. Groups tend to choose to engage in programs that maintain equilibrium and maintain the status quo of status, position, and power. Those with power influence the choice of program. As far back as W. F. Whyte's study, Street-Corner Society, it was noted that status people like to engage in activities in which they excel and they influence the group to select such activities. Power people tend to control the limits of the group horizons by controlling information and communication and, as we have shown, by controlling the available resources for need-meeting. A worker who rationalizes the positive values of a group and assumes that groups are good for all people may be oblivious to a rape of democracy just as we in the past have espoused neutrality in foreign affairs and watched small nations beaten into the ground by aggressors while we sat back and felt virtuous because we refrained from intervening.

Small-group research shows that group life in this country tends to reflect the major society and duplicates interpersonal relations as they exist throughout the culture. A great many "little guys" have suffered the deprivation of love and care as children in their homes and they have been subjected to domination and autocracy in the family and in school. One sees the signs of impinging environments that either have not possessed the resources that foster positive health, or having them, have refused to share them with the members. As a result, some people have grown warped in the making, with ego deficits, with a sense of inadequacy, with atrophy of feeling for others, with guilt, doubt and shame, and with deep hurts and internalized rage. These are the people who, hopefully, come to seek our services and whom we are set up to serve.

The group, left on its own, tends to emulate society by establishing a pecking order and a structure which allocates rewards based upon status, position, and power. Subgroups are formed; some include and some exclude. Those people who need the most are often the ones who are denied access to them. Again, duplicating the macrocosm, they may sell their souls for a smidgeon of acceptance. They conform to the demands of others to buy security and they suppress their creativity, if any is left, in order to gain the transient favor of the few who control the resources. In the hierarchy of needs, the need to belong takes precedence over the need for self-expression; the need not to be ignored hides the need to be wanted; the need to have security supercedes the need to become somebody.

The failure of a social environment to provide

human contact stifles the cry but not the yearning, and the individual seems willing to accept
the imitation version of closeness, the fiction of
groupness, and to pay the price. He tries to meet
the expectation of the role in which he is cast,
in which he is trapped, and in which he is reinforced. His self-image is reinforced and his
littleness is perpetuated.

He has other avenues. There are other choices.
He can act out and be someone to be reckoned with
by virtue of his deviance and violence. He can
cop out and escape through withdrawal. We recall
that Bion called these "fight and flight." He can
also adopt all of the signs of illness, physical
or emotional. By so doing, he can take to his bed,
or at least be able to rationalize his inadequacy
as being caused by a physical impairment, or he
can survive by becoming mentally ill.

Many of these people come to us. The weak and
ineffectual, the isolates and schizoid ones, the
self-defeaters and the passive accepters. They are
in our groups, the drop-outs, the delinquents, the
psychosomatic, and the emotionally disturbed.

Small-group research has alerted us to the
fact that we cannot put them back into groups which
perpetuate the life situations that allowed them
to develop as they have. By and large, most groups
duplicate the social patterns from which these people come. In many instances groups conducted by
well-meaning social workers develop typical group
processes and structures.

Katz and Kahn write, "The peer group is a
promising vehicle for intragroup processes of influence because equal status and power encourage
full discussion, free decision-making, and the internalization of the resulting decisions. Research
evidence clearly establishes the effectiveness of
such group discussion and decision-making in changing behavior and attitudes where the individual is
the target of the attempts to produce change."[1] We
know from small-group theory that equal status and
power and free decision-making in typical groups

---

[1]Katz and Kahn, The Social Psychology of
Organization, p. 396.

are myths. It is indeed the function of the group-worker to enable them to come to pass.

The implication throughout is that social workers apply the knowledge of group process and use the group to achieve stated objectives. We are offered the knowledge about small groups and are encouraged to apply it to social work practice. In effect, this means manipulating group factors. It suggests that the worker intervene and maneuver the group process. This is not the most helpful formulation for our present times.

The value of small-group theory to the worker is that it helps him to be able to share what goes on in the group with the group, to face the members with the realities of their operation, to foster a climate in which they can express their yearnings, needs, disappointments, and frustrations and decide freely whether they approve of exploitation. The other-role is made more explicit, and empathy and self-awareness meld. If they are free and if what happens is their own responsibility, the power that lies within the group can be channeled into mutual aid and into the will and skill to change a society that creates groups in its own pattern.

Bibliography for Small Group Theory

Hubert Bonner, Group Dynamics: Principles and Applications, New York: Ronald Press, 1959).

D. Cartwright and A. Zander, Group Dynamics, Research and Theory, Evanston, Ill.: Row Peterson & Co., 2nd Ed., 1960.

P. Hare, E. F. Borgatta, R. F. Bales, Small Groups: Studies in Social Interaction, New York: Alfred A. Knopf, 1955.

George C. Homans, Social Behavior, Its Elementary Forms, New York: Harcourt, Brace, and World, 1961.

David Katz and Robert L. Kahn, The Social Psychology of Organizations, New York: John Wiley & Sons, 1966.

N. J. Smelzer and W. T. Smelzer (eds.), Personality and Social Systems, New York: John Wiley & Sons, 1963.

Edwin J. Thomas (ed.), Behavioral Science for Social Workers, New York: The Free Press, 1967.

CHAPTER 10

CRITIQUE OF SOCIAL RESEARCH

A well-known characteristic of social workers is our self-debasing attitude and our unwillingness to defend ourselves when attacked. Lately, it has become quite popular to scapegoat social work and most of the attacks, while each contains a grain of truth, are unjustified. For instance, it has become fashionable for politicians and policy makers to declare that welfare is in a mess and that the social services must be completely overhauled. That there is a need for a revision of the delivery of service systems is undoubtedly true, but it is not true, as alleged, that social workers are to blame for their anachronistic organizations, the paltry welfare payments, or the perpetuation of poverty. Social workers do not make policy and have not designed the social service structure.

Social workers have persistently called for revisions and improvements in social welfare organizations and have presented to legislatures, year after year, plans and designs for more modern methods of meeting the problems of the times. The outmoded structures and the restricted dimensions of social welfare have been perpetuated by inadequate funds, staff shortages, and unsympathetic public opinion. It is true that we have accepted these conditions but we have not been responsible for them. The ineffectiveness and inefficiency of the welfare system have been kept so by those who make policy.

The clients also criticize social work and have suggested that social work has helped to maintain poverty and keep the client group in a state of dependence. The practitioner is considered fair game for the attack while boards, chest directorates, and the voting public go scott-free. The American people really do not support good social services, and social work is a convenient scapegoat to assuage the guilt of the giving public and safely release the anger and frustration of the client.

How is it that social workers are willing to accept the scapegoat role and rarely, if ever, answer back? Is it inherent in the personalities of those who choose the profession? Social workers react like a typical minority group. They seem to agree that if everyone says social workers are a worthless group, it must be so or else why would they say it. Social work seems to develop a self-hate attitude and almost gleefully takes up the cry of the majority in loudly announcing its sins and deficits.

One notes that as soon as a politician, a newsworthy figure, or a news story attacks social work, one of our own profession rises to repeat the invective and to say that we must repent and make amends. The conferees at the 1969 National Conference of Social Welfare, for example, applauded loudly every time a critic made a castigating remark from the floor or platform.

Social work has been under constant attack from social researchers and, especially, social scientists who allege that social work lacks theory, that it is unscientific, and that it has not subjected its operations to careful research. While there is some truth in these assessments, those who attack social work for such failings are not free of similar deficits in their own disciplines.

There is a fundamental difference between the knowledge base of a discipline and that of a profession.[1] A profession bases practice on an operational or middle theory. Our mission lies in helping people and, therefore, the kind of theory we need and the research that must be done to validate it differ markedly from the prescriptions in the social sciences.[2] For this and other reasons, social work should not be emulating social science research in its selection of problems to be solved or methods to be employed. Social workers must

---

[1]Peter L. Berger, *Invitation to Sociology: Humanistic Perspective* (Garden City, N. Y.: Doubleday & Co., Inc., 1963).

[2]Catherine S. Chilman, "Production of New Knowledge of Relevance to Social Work and Social Welfare: An Examination of Practice and Curriculum," *Social Work Education Reporter* (September, 1969), 49-54.

develop and fashion research methods that are specific to practice problems and which will answer practice questions effectively.

At this writing the staff of at least one large, national funding agency is divided down the middle around questions of research design and methods. At least one-half of the leading researchers in that agency are contending that the social research methodology which is considered to be standard has not proven itself to be productive in the social professions. A substantial group goes further and alleges that the usual prescriptions for social research, in fact, inhibit the successful obtaining of useful knowledge for practice in the helping professions. The overall conclusion would seem to be that the classical models and methods devised by sociologists are not wholly applicable or appropriate in the search for truth.

The people who are advocating new approaches in social research object to such things as the ritualistic observance of the use of control groups, the narrowly defined and narrowly conceived variables of which some are assumed to remain constant, the simple cause and effect designs, the statistical analysis and the insistence upon rigid mathematical measurements, and so on.

The researchers who are arguing for new approaches to find a method that is more appropriate to social science are few in number. The social science coterie and, especially, the sociologists are wedded to their designs. Social research method in its usual form has not produced nearly what it should or could have had method not been deified. The results that have been obtained through federal grants in the social sciences have been small in relation to the time and money spent.

Maas, who has been a supporter of the application of social science knowledge to social work, as well as a researcher and interpreter of social research, has concluded that their yields in terms of utility in social work practice have been very disappointing. He raises many questions about the viability of current social research methods and suggests that our profession needs to re-examine its research stance which has been modeled on theory-testing social science instead of being based upon designs for producing guides to action.[1]

What seems to have taken place is that social researchers have become so enamored of their method that method has become the determining factor in any project instead of the search for truth. This is a good example of goal displacement and ritualism.

Social workers have been led to believe that social research methods that have been developed in the social sciences are scholarly and excellent, that they are applicable to social work research, and that the knowledge which has been imputed to such methods is both reliable and applicable to social work practice. All of these attributes are open to serious doubt.[2] Not only does social work believe these questionable allegations, but in its low self-image, it fills research faculty posts in schools of social work with social scientists, giving high preference to doctoral degrees in the social-science-research orientations. Many schools promote the idea that social work doctoral students should take courses in social science departments. This conduct tends to stabilize affairs so that the status quo is insured and perpetuated.

Several deleterious outcomes accrue from these policies. Social work students learn only research methods which are inappropriate to social work, the quality of social work research is kept low, and students are convinced that there is more value in research which can tell one the state of things as they are than in seeking ways that aim at bettering them. Hence, students in masters' programs are reinforced as to the importance of seeking knowledge, facts, data, and analytical tools for their own sake. They are discouraged from doing studies in social work method and in applications of knowledge to practice, and are supported in the belief that social workers are vague and unscientific. In addition, as a by-product, students are

---

[1]Henry S. Maas, "Social Work, Knowledge and Social Responsibility," Journal of Education for Social Work (Spring, 1968), 37-48.

[2]N. R. Yarrow, S. D. Campbell and R. V. Burton, Child Rearing: An Inquiry into Research and Methods (San Francisco: Jossey-Bass, Inc., 1968).

taught that "it is impossible to assess certain social phenomena because we do not have the instruments," meaning that the research method is more important than trying to solve problems with the available resources. This kind of reasoning effectively inhibits social workers who do not have research sophistication from attempting to study the problems that vitally concern them. When the student receives his master's degree and graduates, he eschews research.

We have been led to believe that present social research methods are synonymous with scientific inquiry and scholarship. Rigid methodology does not necessarily produce scholarship and one should be very careful not to confuse mechanical, technical sophistication with creativity and depth. I reviewed a study this year that was comparable to the most exquisite example of the watchmaker's art for its mechanical excellence and precision. It was like a beautiful piece of chronography which would have kept time to within a second for a month. However, the researcher had begun with a faulty set of premises and, consequently, arrived at faulty conclusions, despite the excellence of his device.

Real scholarship seeks the truth and is engaged in solving problems, explaining phenomena, and discovering that which is new. These attributes have not characterized social research to date. Fred L. Polak, a Dutch social scientist, in Mankind 2000, castigates the contemporary social sciences as "passive and sterile, rigid and frigid." He wants generalists to aid social scientists in creating a future-oriented society aware of the choices to be made and the reasons for and against a proposed course of action.[1] It is for precisely the same reasons that I think social workers are needed to guide the research for social work.

Much of the knowledge base in the social sciences which purports to rest upon social research is not reliable for social work practice.[2] Social

---

[1]R. Jungk and J. Galtung, Mankind 2000 (Oslo: Universitetsforlaget, 1968).

[2]Yarrow, Campbell, and Burton, Child Rearing: An Inquiry into Research and Methods.

research methods, as currently taught and practiced, generally speaking, are inappropriate to
social work with groups for the following reasons:

1. Groups in the laboratory, or groups of
students in a psychology course are not real-life
groups and, hence, conclusions which are drawn
from studying them are inapplicable to our practice. There are very few studies of practice
groups. Very few of the findings in small group
research have been tested in real life or practice
and little has been subjected to inquiry with real-
life problems or in the realm of social work realities.

2. Social research usually concludes with
probabilities about averages and percentages about
categories of people or problems which are not necessarily valid for a given case or a specific group
in practice.

3. The social sciences do not provide reliable
findings from which one can generalize and often
confuse theory with fact. In addition, much that
is reported is only observation and description;
many of the findings are obvious; and there is a
paucity of explanation.

4. The tendency is to develop categories, or
labels and force the findings to fit into them.
People and their problems do not fit neatly into
cubbyholes.

5. The social researcher tries to generalize
from large populations to groups or individuals;
this is not valid. On other occasions he general-
izes from small units to large ones; this is equally
invalid.

6. Research findings in the social sciences
tend to be applicable more readily to policy or program or similar broad propositions than to practice
with individuals or groups.

7. When studying the effects of social work
the social researcher tends not to spell out the
method variables, misstates them, or misapplies
them.

The Girls at Vocational High study was cited
earlier. The purpose was not to criticize that

study specifically but to use it as a typical example. One could make the same points with a more recent study of multi-problem families.[1] In the first study, the authors sought to assess the effectiveness of social casework. They utilized a model of casework which most social caseworkers reject and generalized from this to all casework. They disregarded the setting and system as a possible determinant of the outcome; they implied voluntary involvement of the girls which was not entirely so; they did not stay within the context of the theory within which the practice was conducted; and several competent reviewers were able to deduce different conclusions which means that there was a reasonable doubt.

These researchers are very able and respected and have been engaged in research for many years. One has to believe that they must have known of all the flaws that have been mentioned. Norman Herstein suggests that the researchers were hostile to social work and were not committed to finding the truth.[2] One might ask whether all social researchers are ethical.

8. Social researchers mask or mat the area of inquiry so that only the section which they want to look at can be seen. In the Girls High study the agency as an impinging environment was masked out.

Mario D. Fantini has uncovered another example of the masking of evidence. In reviewing several books about the culturally deprived child and compensatory education, he observes that many published studies seek to demonstrate that the slow learner in public school is deficient because of family circumstances, cultural deprivation, inadequacy of stimulation in infancy, poor diet, low IQ, or personality defects. The researchers care-

---

[1]Lyndell Scott, book review of The Multi-Problem Dilemma: A Social Research Demonstration with Multi-Problem Families appearing in Social Service Review (June, 1969), 215-16.

[2]Norman Herstein, "The Latent Dimension of Social Work Research," Social Casework (May, 1969), 269-75.

fully masked out the inadequacies of the school system, the curriculum, the teaching method, and other impinging environmental factors.[1]

9. Social researchers consider it proper when seeking to solve a large and complex problem to work on a small part of it at a time. With simple cause-and-effect dynamics such a procedure might be productive; in flat terms, one might complete a jigsaw puzzle in this fashion but as soon as one views social phenomena in systems terms, working on small parts in an attempt to understand the whole or even some of the parts no longer works. If one seeks to understand how a person behaves in a group, simple correlations of a few variables lead to erroneous findings. Social work practice deals with complex and multi-faceted-systems relationships. Social researchers like to examine single or at best small numbers of variables at one time, and most often when not in interaction. The results are unreliable.

10. It is not unusual to find research designs which ignore large numbers of facts. This can have been done for convenience, or can have been a rationalization that the omitted facts were irrelevant, it can have been an oversight, or it can have been an unwillingness to reveal certain facts.

11. Also, in many social research studies, there is a more subtle failure to reveal basic assumptions and beliefs which the researcher holds. It seems that when the researcher wants to prove a point, he can start with assumptions that will predetermine the end result. Removing the stigma of conscious motivation to reach certain conclusions, the fact remains that there are biases, beliefs, and assumptions in all of us.

In many studies the assumption of the researcher is hidden as, for example, a recent study which sought to determine Jewish identification patterns in Jewish centers. The researcher used as criteria, attendance at Sunday school and observances of re-

---

[1] Mario D. Fantini, "Beyond Cultural Deprivation and Compensatory Education," <u>Psychiatric and Social Science Review</u> (June, 1969).

ligious rituals. He assumed that these measured
identification. Not only was he mistaken, but he
failed to set forth his assumptions for examination
by the reader.

12. Abraham Kaplan distinguishes between research conducted within the context of discovering
and that conducted within the context of justification. The first seeks ideas and the second attempts
to prove ideas.[1] There is all too little seeking
and there are all too many attempts to prove pre-
conceptions and biases in social research.

13. Reading social research reports in the
literature one often finds a failure of the dis-
closed facts to support the stated conclusions beyond a reasonable doubt and, in addition there is
unconvincing logic and omissions of evidence. An
adversary system such as the chemists' association
uses might prevent many such reports from being
published as the social researcher would have to
submit his work to argument by his peers before it
was printed.

Social researchers are more interested in research than in truth. My primary training before
becoming a social worker was in law. It is a
function of a lawyer to elicit all of the facts in
a given case and to assemble these facts so that
they add up to conclusions "beyond a reasonable
doubt." A lawyer is trained to examine the entire
case and he must fit every fact into the reasoning
that supports his conclusions or account for every
fact that does not. He is not privileged to ignore certain facts or to focus his inquiry in such
a way as to view only part of the case. A lawyer
must be an expert in logic and in the laws of evidence because if he is not his opponent will be
and will fault him.

The validity of any argument is tested through
the adversary system. Any fact that a lawyer omits
will be brought up by his adversary, and any lax-
ness in his logic will be seized upon at once.
Social workers have been remiss in not challenging

---

[1]Abraham Kaplan, The Conduct of Inquiry:
Methodology for Behavioral Science (San Francisco:
Chandler Publishing Co., 1965).

the research findings and conclusions reported to them which have proven to be erroneous when tested in practice or when subjected to scrutiny for omissions and found to violate the laws of validation and logic.

14. Much that needs to be done in practice cannot be measured or quantified. Evaluative procedures must be predicated upon a different set of criteria than that which the researchers currently honor.

15. Sociologists, when they engage in research, often forget their own theories and operate as though a large organizational change would alter the attitudes and needs of the members and as though changes in attitudes and role performances in individual members would effect changes in large organizations in socially desirable ways.

16. Social science research ignores "oughts" and is less interested in change than in describing what is being examined.

17. It is of concern that the social scientists usually do not know what questions to ask in social work or how to ask them. When social workers tell them what they need to find out, they often skew the studies to what they think are the important questions but these may not be of use to social work. We need to free ourselves from the fetters of social research methods and begin to devise social work research methods, to train creative social work researchers, and to go after the questions that need answering in an orderly sequence from the simple to the complex. Many complex studies are undertaken in the group field without a firm base because one has not yet been developed for that particular study and the researcher is not willing to do first things first.

Everything that has been said about the inadequacies of social science researchers does not in any way excuse social workers. I am not for a moment letting us off that easily, but rather, I am telling the social science people that the things of which they accuse us are true of them as well. One must give credit where credit is due; at least they are trying to do research.

However, whatever inadequacies there are in

social research today and however valid the contention that social work ought not to emulate these unprofitable methods, the fact remains that social work must begin to study systematically the phenomena and the problems which are clearly within its system boundaries and design ways of making the necessary investigations. We have been made to believe that research method has a hierarchy of statuses. Collecting and collating is said to be very low level, that is, not "in." But we are at a level of knowledge and practice in groupwork that requires collecting and collating. We need to know what are the different kinds of groups and what are the significant differences in the ways in which they function. There is the important question of composition; what kinds of composition (members) effect what kind of group functioning?

For example, we need to collect facts about what kinds of problems groups have and what kinds of individual problems are related to what kinds of group problems. We need to collect facts about the kinds of workers and the kinds of methods found in groupwork. We need these facts before, I emphasize before, we can formulate hypotheses or start to study correlations, and surely before we can begin to assess methods of practice.

Research in groupwork must proceed in some orderly fashion so that we can develop sounder systems of practice based upon the knowledge of the specific conditions under which specific behaviors will change in specific directions. Once we have some sound information about these factors, we can study the question of what methods produce what changes in what situations.

As of now, social researchers have studied groups and addressed themselves to group factors as though each were independent at one time and then a dependent variable at another. This is not profitable for the groupworker. We have sought to assess method without knowing the worker or without carefully analyzing the setting. The scientists tell us we cannot study all these variables in interaction. When you work with a group you have to take all of them into account, so it is hopeless to say it cannot be done.

It cannot be done with the fine, calibrated

instruments they want to use and with the precision they require. The Aztecs produced a calendar[1] and a time science based upon their observations of the heavens with the crudest of instruments made of stone. They collected and collated facts discernible to the naked eye and about which they used their intelligence. They learned of the relationship of the stars to the seasons, and by so doing, the basic dynamics of astronomy. We will be able to know much more about groups than we do now if we divest ourselves of fancy instrumentation and get down to study. This must be done first as a preparation for more sophisticated studies later. What kind of worker can effect what kind of results, with what kind of problems, in what kind of group, in what kind of setting, using what kinds of methods? The ultimate in our work lies in specifics.

One might get the impression in this chapter that I am anti-science and anti-research. I am neither. I am anti-dogma and against the kinds of restrictive rituals which stifle creativity and scholarship. There cannot be only one way to solve a problem, to design a study, to elicit the facts, to discover the correlations, or to explain the phenomena. This is what makes living so exciting and being a student so stimulating. I am against those who want to pretend that it is all cut and dried, mechanical, technical, and that it always conforms to a mathematical formula. I am opposed to the idea of any standardized research method; I am interested in how to find solutions to problems.

Research in our field can be an experience in discovery, one as fascinating as those early years when, as children, we were spellbound by the wonder of it all until our teachers and schools washed the stars out of our eyes and taught us not to be curious and to conform. We are confronted with the same unhappy situation in many schools of social work. Students enroll with great anticipation, a sense of adventure and exploration. Soon the stars are no longer there. It is no secret that the coup de grace often is given by the research faculty who are wont to infuse the atmosphere with rigid procedures instead of creative scholarship. The job of discovery becomes an exercise in conformation.

---

[1]The Sun Stone.

I have written this book with the wish that you be spared the disappointments of trampled curiosity and trammeled imagination, and with the hope that when you work with people you will always strive to help them to be free, to grow, and to achieve the heights to which they are capable.

INDEX OF AUTHORS

ABOUT THE AUTHOR

Alan F. Klein is Professor of Social Work at the School of Social Welfare, State University of New York at Albany, where he is responsible for curriculum development. For eight years he was chairman of the Social Groupwork specialization at the University of Pittsburgh Graduate School of Social Work and later became chairman of the Human Growth and Social Environment sequence. In 1964-65, after returning from sixteen months in Hong Kong where he directed a team developing social work education, he created one of the first comprehensive human growth sequences successfully integrating social and cultural content with broadly based psychological knowledge.

From 1947 to 1955, while teaching at the School of Social Work of the University of Toronto, he achieved an international reputation as an authority in social groupwork and also in community recreation and camping.

For the last few years, he has been in practice as a family group counselor at Technoma-Craig House, a treatment center for families of emotionally disturbed children. He studied family group counseling as part of a team with a three-year N. I.M.H. grant and later conducted a research study in group methods in institutions for acting-out adolescents with a special grant from the State of Pennsylvania.

His practice experience includes social settlements, Jewish centers, and children's clinics. For many years, he has been consultant and training advisor on group methods for the Veterans Administration.

Among his previous publications are <u>Society, Democracy, and the Group</u>, <u>Role Playing</u>, and <u>The Effective Use of Role Playing</u> along with countless pamphlets, journal articles, papers, and films. He holds degrees of Juris Doctor, Master of Social Work, and Bachelor of Science in Social Science.